ARE YOU POSSESSED?

Now is the Time for Divine Intervention!

Wayne Brewer & Arianna Nappi

Edited by: Josh Brenton
Cover Design by: Ryan Ratliff: www.rrwebandgraphicdesign.com

Printed in the United States of America
ISBN: 978-0-578-03923-7
ISBN: 978-0-9856133-1-0

Library of Congress Control Number: 2009941918

Published by
Wayne Brewer
11024 Montgomery Blvd. NE, No. 260
Albuquerque, NM 87111
Website: www.AreYouPossessed.net

To:

Archangel Raphael,

Archangel Michael,

and

Jesus Christ

TABLE OF CONTENTS

DEMON DETECTIVE

The phone rings late at night, just as Wayne is settling into bed. A familiar, but panic-stricken voice on the other end tells him there's a super-natural emergency occurring in her living room and seconds later, Wayne runs out the door. At the chaotic scene, he sees a woman lying on the floor—weeping, writhing in pain—crying out "It hurts! It hurts!" Her friends are standing around her sending loving energy, trying desperately to help, but to no avail. When Wayne walks in, everyone steps back to make room for him as if he were a surgeon entering a room full of nurses and medical techs.

Instead of carrying a black leather bag with scissors and scalpels, Wayne brings with him 100,000 angels and his team of guides: Jesus Christ, Archangel Raphael and Archangel Michael. He immediately begins to work, placing his hands under the woman's head and asking his angelic team to cleanse her body of the entities causing the pain. Michael and Raphael begin pushing and pulling the dark creatures out of her convulsing body—then she's quiet and still. Witnessing Jesus enter the woman's physical form to fill her with Love and Light, Wayne knows by her euphoric grin that she has received the grace of a Divine Healing. . . and so does she.

As a private investigator (PI), it has been Wayne's job for the last thirty-four years to seek the truth. He's good at his job because he works by the philosophy that a person is guilty until proven innocent; that a claim is fraudulent until proven authentic. This has served him well professionally and it is this discernment that has benefited him in discovering the truth regarding channeling, Divine Healings and the existence of spirits among us.

Wayne grew up on his family's farm in Iowa. It was a much simpler life compared to the one most of us are accustomed to living in today's insidiously fast-paced, technologically advanced world. Wayne began helping on the farm at an early age and during one bright, August day when he was only five-years-old, he was assisting the tractor in moving one dozen bales of hay via the use of a pulley system that was designed to move the hay high into the barn. When his left hand got caught in a pulley, he received a rope burn so deep the scar remains with him to this day. Now, more than fifty years later, he uses this same, scarred hand for the purpose of spiritually *pulling* entities and other dark energies from his clients.

Wayne's memory of being touched by the grace and mercy of the Divine commences during his teenage years. He was still in high school when he had his first conscious, experiential awareness of angelic activity in his life. It happened during a rather foolish excursion he and his cousin initiated on a tractor after walking and cutting the weeds out of the long rows of soybeans.

With his cousin at the wheel, the two boys raced across the field, pushing the tractor as fast as it could go toward Wayne's older brother, Tom, and a neighbor, who were waiting at the other end. They swerved back and forth as if they were in a high-performance race car. They intended to stop at just the last moment, scaring Tom and the neighbor in a way they had never encountered!

As they sped closer to the other boys, Wayne *knew* that he had to move off of the rear axle on which he was standing and down onto the hitch behind the driver's seat as the tractor plowed ahead at full-speed: twenty-five miles per hour... he just didn't know why. With sophomoric enthusiasm he eagerly anticipated the look on his brother's face after they stopped only inches away. What he didn't anticipate was his cousin deliberately jamming his foot on the brake for the left wheel—locking it in place and causing the tractor to roll upside-down—instantaneously; incomprehensibly quick for such a heavy piece of equipment!

Wayne remembers that morning very clearly, "My cousin never slowed down. As we got toward the end of the field, we went down a little hill and he sharply turned the tractor and locked the left wheel at the last second, and the tractor flipped... just then somebody picked me up... just picked me up from the back of my neck, just lifted me off that tractor. I just knew it; knew that it was an angel! It just lifted me off that tractor and set me on the ground running full-speed... and I saw the tractor flip over and my cousin go underneath it... and watched it land on top of him. I never stopped; I just kept right on running to get help... that was my first experience with angels."

3

After a lengthy hospitalization and rehabilitation, his cousin recovered from his serious injuries and Wayne turned his attention skyward. By the time he was sixteen, he was licensed as a solo-pilot. He loved pretending to be a fighter pilot, diving down close enough to people on the ground to see the whites of their eyes, pulling up so tightly that the wheels on his single-engine plane brushed the leaves of the trees.

A couple of years later, Wayne registered at a college in Iowa to obtain a degree that would meet the requirements of joining the Air Force and fulfill his dream of becoming a fighter pilot. At this time he had no awareness of his past lives and did not realize he was attempting to live one of them again.

Although he intuitively knew that going to war in Vietnam as a fighter pilot would be the last thing he ever did, Wayne pushed forward with this ill-fated, militaristic intention. But it seemed that the Universe had other plans. While playing in a baseball game during his first year in college, he literally snapped—broke his left femur—creating two bones in his thigh instead of one. This injury immediately disqualified him for military service during an era that had an abundance of young men willing to lay down their lives for their country. He was hospitalized for more than six weeks while in traction: and staring out the window at a brick wall, gave eighteen-year-old Wayne plenty of time to reconsider his secular path.

Like many young students, Wayne changed his direction in college too. He began with the intent to obtain a degree in Finance but decided to study Theology and Religion. This deep inner desire to reconnect with the Divine was a driving force for Wayne's growth. It helped him to realize that the depth of the connection he was searching for was not one he could find in religious doctrine. He learned that he didn't want a mediator between himself and God, but simply to "tap in, tune in, and turn on."

In January of 1992, Wayne endured a third injury that once again affected the left side of his body. During a ski jump on one of his favorite slopes, something went terribly awry and when he landed, he broke his left humerus—the long bone in the arm extending from the shoulder to the elbow—and he also fractured the ball in his shoulder socket in twelve places. Fortunately, he was skiing with a group of friends that included several nurses and they helped the only doctor in town reset the bone after Wayne was hauled off the mountain with his fractured arm still distorted above his head. It was after the healing of this injury that Wayne's left arm occasionally began to twitch.

It was understandable that Wayne believed he had sustained some neurological damage in his left arm that would cause it to twitch when he relaxed or entered a meditative state. Considering this a lingering symptom from healed injuries, Wayne did not place much emphasis, or worry about its implications; it was not impacting his life in any significant way... not until April 2008, when he received a book called *The Secret* from a friend named Luz.

Luz and Wayne have known each other for a very long time: they have spent at least four lifetimes together prior to this one. After reading *The Secret,* Wayne was interested in learning more about basic metaphysical practices and principles, for example, how to meditate and the significance of past life experiences. In fact, it appeared to Wayne that their lifetimes of deep spiritual bonds coupled with Luz's intention to share with him an enlightened teaching, is what really motivated him to explore.

From this starting point, Wayne's investigative nature moved him to read more on the subject, including channeled works by Abraham through Jerry and Esther Hicks. Specifically, a book titled *The Law of Attraction*, which states, *"That which is like unto itself is drawn."*

Wayne recounts how highly skeptical he was of this information, "I almost threw the Abraham book away after the first chapter because it went against everything I was taught… channeling spirits?"

Wayne's logical PI mind combined with his traditional Christian background and training, rejected these possibilities at first glance. What was it that made Wayne keep reading through the resistance of his ego mind? He intuitively knew the book was channeled and in his heart, he could *feel* that the information came from a higher source. And *feeling* is a fundamental part of understanding how to use "the secret" to create the life you desire.

The Secret and *The Law of Attraction* are books that reveal a fundamental law of the Universe that governs life and experience. The Law of Attraction holds that every thought has its own vibration, and coded within this vibration is an asking of the Universe to deliver to you experiences that match your thoughts.

By paying attention to what you think and how it correlates with what you feel, you will find the key to the Law of Attraction. You will begin to notice that God and the Universe are giving you what you ask for by responding to what you think about! The implications of this are astounding! If the Universe matches your thoughts and gives you what you think about whether you want it or not, all you have to do to draw to yourself the experiences you desire is think about and focus on what you *do* want.

How do you know if you're changing your habits of thinking successfully? All you have to do is *feel* it! Your emotions are an indication of the frequency your thoughts are transmitting. If you feel good emotions such as: love, appreciation, joy and gratitude, you are sending out high frequency thoughts and creating more things that feel good. If you feel bad emotions such as: unhappiness, depression, sadness and worry, you are sending out thoughts of a low vibration or frequency and thus creating more things that will match your negative emotions.

In *practice*, the use of the Law of Attraction is a powerful way, as Abraham expresses, to get "tapped in, tuned in, and turned on" to your own beautiful connection with your higher power. In *practice*, it is a powerful way to attract to yourself the experiences you want, rather than simply being at the mercy of your own unconscious thinking patterns, which are your patterns of asking by default without knowledge of this law!

Being a logical person and one trained in finding hidden truth, Wayne did not immediately conclude that he was having a spiritual—not a physical—experience as his arm twitched from the downloading of energy he was receiving during his meditative states. He believed that there might be some neurological issues and started researching this possibility.

For Wayne to even consider any other viewpoint regarding his involuntary arm movement beyond nerve damage, something profound had to occur. Something undeniable. Something that could not possibly be justified by his traditionally Western thought process on the matter.

Imagine Wayne's surprise and amazement one evening when he settled into bed to do some reading and the normal quivering sensation in his arm suddenly blossomed into wild flailing! As a psychic, I, Arianna, am privileged with the ability to "look into" a matter and my Spiritual Guides show me images that are relevant to the issue at hand. What I saw in these visions was the following: Wayne sitting in bed, reading a book and an angel gently grabbing him by his left wrist, raising it in an arc, back and forth over Wayne's bed; his arm swinging from side-to-side like the most emphatic wave imaginable but with enough force to tug Wayne *across* his bed.

The angels chuckled and rejoiced because this was no longer a phenomenon Wayne could write-off as a physical symptom! Knowing that there was no doctor he could see that would give him a logical explanation of what was happening to him, Wayne set his intention to find the truth behind his experience.

Now that Wayne was prompted to look beyond the world of Western medicine, he felt compelled to investigate other possibilities and in December 2008, went to see a well-known psychic and Channel based in Albuquerque, New Mexico: Betsy-Morgan Coffman. Wayne had been seeing her advertisements in various newspapers for more than twenty years. Betsy, whose contact information is listed on the *Resources* page at the end of this book, channels information from the higher realms for her clients; information regarding the past, present and future.

It was Wayne's first, close encounter with a psychic and he went in with the same attitude he utilizes to investigate matters for his clients: guilty until proven innocent; fraudulent until proven legitimate. He took none of the information provided at face value; he merely collected it and waited to see if it proved true. He was not interested in easy answers; just the truth.

During this session with Betsy, it was explained to Wayne that there were several important past lifetimes that were coming into play in his current incarnation. He had lived during the time Jesus was on the planet and he learned the truth of Jesus' teachings, integrating them deeply into himself and becoming a teacher of truth. In that incarnation, Wayne knew Jesus well and in his heart. In another lifetime, Wayne was a samurai who studied under a master teacher that taught him that truth and integrity are to be honored above all else—and how the mind, body and spirit blend together. He was also a fighter pilot during World War II that hated war and never returned home alive.

Naturally, Wayne asked Betsy and her guides if they could explain what was happening with his left arm and to his surprise and embarrassment he was told by Betsy and her primary guide, Orion, "You are a spiritual being. That left arm is filled with energy. You are bringing through Light. You knew Jesus and you knew him well in your heart. You've got Christed energy (the energies or frequency of Jesus) in you.... You will do miracles and it is to start this year and you're to do a lot in the next three years to help the planet Earth ascend."

Wayne's left arm was receiving—channeling—very real healing energy: Light. The involuntary jerking movement of his left arm was a wake-up call from the Spiritual Masters who guide him and a response to the energy that was moving through him.

Wayne works with a variety of Master Teaching Guides including: Jesus, John the Baptist and his mentor from his lifetime as a samurai. The presence of Archangel Raphael and Archangel Michael were already at work and involved in this phenomenon. Archangel Raphael is Wayne's primary guide: he is always present, always available and the guide who comes through with messages and healing unless another guide is specifically requested.

Certain people were called, Wayne was told, and his number for service was up, "You have an assignment, you agreed." Betsy continues, "They're saying, '*It's Time.*'"

The agreement referred to above entails the planning we all do at a soul level before we are born into physical form. Wayne was experiencing an amazing, spiritual awakening: to the fact that he is a healer who would channel healings and wisdom from the higher realms.

Orion continues his message for Wayne through Betsy: "This path will begin in the next three months and continue in an escalated fashion for the next three years. You have a gift. When you channel, you'll be able to use this for the offering of miracles, for the channeling of Light...."

As if this declaration of fate was not enough to integrate and emotionally digest, Wayne was also told that he was to take a channeling class, write a book and teach others what he learns! You are holding one of Betsy's predictions in your hands!

"That was my first time with any of this," Wayne recalls. "I was really skeptical. As a PI I'm really skeptical.... Betsy said, 'You will channel,' and I said, 'No I won't.' She said, 'You are going to write a book,' and I said, 'No I'm not.' She told me, 'You're going to be healing... miracles are going to start within the next three months,' and I said, 'Oh yeah, right!' Next thing I know, three weeks later I'm in a channeling class."

Wayne also had no intention of going deeper into channeling by taking advanced classes but that's where he really began to gain an understanding of his tremendous gift and what he was being called to do with it.

In April 2009 I, Arianna, had the privilege of taking the Channeling Level-Three Class (C-3) with Wayne under the instruction of Betsy. Each of us truly enjoyed the unique gift of witnessing each others' growth as our guides appeared and our gifts unfolded before our eyes.

At this advanced level, the Channel becomes integrated with the guides and the frequency begins to unlock other gifts that had previously lain dormant. Wayne was discovering his gifts of healing and the existence of entities. I was discovering that I had the ability to see, or receive visions called "psychic hits."

Until this point in early April, my visions had been like a snapshot of information regarding my own personal growth and healing process but a new vision had surfaced that I found quite disturbing. When I asked the guides what it was and what to do about it, they told me that it was indeed very real, it was malevolent, it was separate from me but living inside and that Wayne could assist in its removal.

At the end of a channeling class with Betsy, we usually hold hands and close with a prayer. I happened to have been sitting next to Wayne on his left side that evening, and when we held hands I felt a surge of energy race up my arm and into my chest cavity where this entity was anchored. In my head I could hear it screaming and I was stunned. I turned to Wayne and asked him if he would help me get rid of this monster that was living inside of me, and he humbly agreed to try.

What I didn't know then was that Wayne, at that point in his spiritual evolution, did not believe in the existence of entities, and certainly not his ability to remove them. He did not experience the surge of energy that I had when we held hands and he thought it was all in my head, but graciously agreed to see me anyway! I also didn't realize that the night we "held hands" was the beginning of Passover: the day the world celebrates Jesus' sacrifices, his willingness to be crucified.

The next night was Thursday and Wayne performed his first entity removal. Please reference the chapter titled *Maria* for a detailed account of how this amazing healing transpired. My appointment was Saturday and Wayne still thought I was crazy until he "laid hands" on me and the angelic team went to work. Immediately and intuitively, Wayne knew what had to be done!

It is remarkable that Wayne truly awoke to his amazing capacity to heal others and release spirits during Passover. Wayne saw the power of healing that emerged through him via the loving presence of Jesus Christ at a time when millions of people were acknowledging Jesus' sacrifices in his earthly form.

All of the names of the individuals that have allowed their experiences to be shared as cases within this book have been changed to protect their privacy. The stories written in this book have been compiled with the use of audio tapes recorded during their sessions, combined with interviews conducted by me, Arianna. Quotations have been edited for content and readability only.

In the interest of giving you a more fulfilling experience and greater understanding as you explore the information contained within these pages, it is prudent to discuss Wayne's process when he facilitates a Divine Healing. While Wayne has assistance from many guides and angels, he primarily works with the energies of Jesus Christ, Archangel Michael and Archangel Raphael. Of these three, only Jesus actually goes inside of the person being healed, filling them with the Love and Light of God.

This *seemingly* presents a dilemma for those who are not of the Christian faith. We use the word seemingly because in reality, <u>you do not need to be Christian. You do not need to accept Jesus as your Savior. You do not even have to like him!</u> All that is required is that you give your permission for Jesus' entry; even he respects your free will! He does not remain in the body forever; just long enough to fill the void and finish the repairs that can only be done from the inside. **These healings are <u>not</u> for the chosen few; they are for everybody!**

While a typical session with Wayne and his healing team may only last one-half hour, he states, "Once I make these appointments, the process really starts at that point in time because a lot of these entities will go to great lengths to keep the individual from coming."

Entities that are going to be removed and sent to the Light are aware of the appointments made by their hosts and will resist by any means at their disposal: including finding ways to prevent their host from arriving at their appointment. Some of their common tactics involve making their hosts feel ill, emptying gas tanks and putting literal obstructions in their path, such as excessive traffic or construction. A portion of Wayne's preparation is devoted to sending spiritual or angelic protection to his incoming clients so they arrive safely and on time.

The dark beings pending removal often engage Wayne on or before the day of the appointment—their energy often produces stomach sickness or nausea for Wayne—that intensifies as the appointment draws near. Preparation for a healing takes a minimum of one hour while Wayne brings forward all of the cleansing, protection and guardianship necessary, but sometimes Wayne begins working on his clients' behalf several days in advance.

In Wayne's words, "You don't just go in and start doing this without being fully armed. It's not you that can arm yourself; they [the angels and guides] have to do it."

It is imperative that inexperienced practitioners do not try this at home. While Wayne may frequently make this look easy, more is required than simply calling in the correct parties. The practitioner must proceed without fear or doubt, as entities feed on this energy and it will make the practitioner vulnerable. Furthermore, the practitioner must be able to hold the extremely high frequency of the angelic team for a long enough and uninterrupted period of time to accomplish the objective. The ability to hold a frequency that high, for that long, takes time and intent to develop; every level of the human being: physical, mental, emotional and spiritual must gradually adjust to higher frequencies. *There is no room for trial and error in this work.*

It is our sincere desire that you find answers in this book. Whatever your experiences have been, there are reasons for it. Some of those reasons may be in your highest good, but some of them may have been caused by an external presence that does not belong in your body, mind, or life. Please keep an open mind as you read through this material and note your reactions as you read. If they are strong in any direction: fear, anger, sadness, joy... you might consider the possibility that you were meant to read this book because it contains a life-changing answer for you. After reading this material, if you think you may have an entity presence in your life, please visit the *Resources* page at the end of this book.

POSSESSION, ENTITIES AND DIVINE HEALINGS

This is the first day of a new life if you want it. It is the beginning of something more joyful, more fulfilling, closer to the true you. Do you know who you are? You are God. You are the fiery fingertips of Divine Light on this planet, this beautiful planet called Earth. You have creative control here. Control over your own life, your experiences, your love and your lessons.

Before further expression and review of the chapters to follow, an explanation of some of the key terms is provided below to help you understand and grasp the profound messages contained within this book. The first term we shall define is channeling. This is a word that scares many, for it has a stigma placed upon it by some groups whose perceptions of reality are defined by human beings.

Let us express and convey now that channeling is Divine! It is the ability to bring forth the Love of God into your body and into your world in profound, energetic ways that may take many forms: words, art, frequency, healing and joy of all dimensions. Like many strengths or attributes, this beautiful gift can be misused to bring forth energies that are not in the Light of God but it will be obvious, for no dark energy

17

can ever measure up to the frequency of Love emitted from a being of Light.

With the gift of channeling—available to all humans—additional gifts will surface such as the third sight, psychic hits or visions. These are received in the sixth chakra, an energy center located just above and between your two physical eyes. You may have previously heard this chakra referred to as the third eye. It can see through the veil of illusion to the future, to the past; without regard for physical distance. It is here that visions described within this book have been seen. These are very personalized to the receiver and often symbolic rather than literal. The viewer knows what he or she is seeing because the symbols used have personal meaning and the visions are accompanied by a frequency, or energy that carries information on the relevance of the vision.

A third eye visual perception of an angel, or of Jesus, may not be what they actually look like but rather a symbol of how the viewer imagines them to be because they do not have physical bodies like humans. These personalized images allow those receiving the visions to know instantly what they are witnessing.

The third eye is susceptible to projections. When a dark being or entity is perceived in the third eye, it often has the ability to project an image of itself in the way it wishes to be perceived. Therefore, a relatively small and low-powered entity may project itself as large and monstrous as a way of scaring those who might wish to banish it from its host and into the Light. Some have no need to project falsely since they have natural forms that might be perceived as frightening to a human being. This is why many healers—such as Wayne—perceive these beings kinesthetically. They *feel* them instead of seeing them.

Let's turn our attention now to entities and possessions. These are not dirty words. Do not fear them. Speaking about these phenomena will promote freedom from the grip they have held over much of humanity throughout history. If humans could acknowledge without fear that these are like common parasites that we have medications and doctors to relieve, the world in which we live would grow lighter and more pleasant.

The greatest defense these dark entities have is your fear. If they can remain hidden, then like a worm in your belly, they can grow and feed on your energy and your power. If they can remain undiscovered, they can manipulate you into feeding them all of the pain, misery, fear and suffering they need to thrive. If you had a worm internally, wouldn't you want to be rid of it? Wouldn't you want to be free and healthy?

The subject of entity possession is not a new one. It has been discussed and expressed throughout history by various cultures living on every continent of our beautiful planet. Only during the modern ages have these truths been covered, hidden: becoming taboo. The descriptions, explanations and information contained herein are a Divinely Guided Account with the purpose of reopening this closed subject of a reality perhaps less pleasant, but just as real as the one you perceive with your five beautiful senses.

Turning away from this subject matter does not make it less true or less real. Pretending that it doesn't exist will not free you from the bindings that such possessions impose upon your precious human experience. Do you not wish to see the truth? To know who you truly are? Don't you desire the freedom to joyously create the life of your dreams?

Possessions are no reflection on you as a person. This is *not* a taboo subject. An entity possession does not make you "bad" or "sinful." It is no indication of your character or values. It is so common that it is almost natural, like catching a flu bug or a cold. When you catch these infections you feel symptoms of the invasion. Possessions are truly comparable, except instead of a runny nose and chest congestion, you may be experiencing negative thoughts, violent images in your mind, or voices that tell you that you're bad, evil or unworthy. Instead of robbing you of your ability to breathe through your nose as a flu virus might, it robs you of your ability to see yourself as you truly are: a vibrant, creative being of unconditional love, loved unconditionally by God.

If you have an entity, you did not get it because you deserved it. You are not being punished by God. It is not because you are bad or evil. It is not the result of a sin you believe you have committed. Do not judge yourself or others. It is as natural to catch an entity as it is to catch the flu.

Here is a very fundamental point to note: when you catch a flu virus you know where to get help; you visit a medical doctor and are given medicine to help your symptoms go away. You can find this doctor by searching the *Yellow Pages* or looking through your health insurance company's Preferred Provider Directory, but what kind of doctor deals with the imbalance of entity possession? This book will offer you great insight on what kind of healer can help with such a "bug." Do you feel ashamed when you see a doctor for the flu? Of course not! So you shouldn't experience any shame if you are hosting an entity; it is just a very curable *dis-ease.*

If entity possession mimics the flu, then cords and attachments are like the common cold. We all have them, for we have been around much longer than we remember. Cords can be compared to ropes. They can be used as binding tools, or restrictive instruments that can keep you from growing or acting upon what your true-self desires. They can also attach you to a past that you do not fully remember, affecting your present life in negative ways. These cords or ropes can be rooted in any part of your physical body—and the other end—can be attached to any person, place or thing in any time-space reality. While you may not be aware that these are present with you, they are impacting your life today.

The healer that can cure this bug is usually not a medical doctor. The healer that can rid you of your symptoms probably won't advertise in the *Yellow Pages*. They may seem somewhat elusive, but be assured that there are many people that are now realizing they can do this work. It is done in a variety of approaches but within this text we are referring to the channeled method because all of the cases mentioned in this book have been healed through this method: Divine Channeled Healings. During a Divine

Healing session, the mighty sword of Archangel Michael can cut these cords so they are no longer attached to anything. These can then be dissolved so that not a trace remains.

There are many forms that entities adopt and not all of them mean you harm but their very presence will cause you suffering whether that is their intention or not. Yes, they have intentions. Yes, they have agendas. And just like you, they are intelligent and conscious.

Sometimes, possessions are initiated by individuals through the use of some common oracular tools that are not fully understood. All of these can be used for Light or for Darkness and uneducated players may inadvertently invite entities of a dark nature. Some common tools include the Ouija Board, or the tarot, or even automatic writing. When these are not used with the proper protection and boundaries, they are unsafe. An example of this is reflected later in this book.

Some entities are simply lost souls who were once human but for one reason or another did not go forth into the Light to be healed and move on with their soul's evolution. These may be termed disincarnate spirits. They stay for a myriad of reasons, some of the most common include the fear of going to hell, attachments to people still living, places, things, and even addictions that they still feel propelled to feed. The addictions and emotions they had in life are still with them because they have retained the same awareness or personal traits that they did when they were in a human body and they will continue to have these until they enter the Light of God.

When disincarnate spirits join a living human in their aura or body, they bring with them all of their attachments, hang-ups, addictions and quirks. These become integrated into the host or embodied human and then influence their thought process, decisions, actions and health. They may have meant you no harm, but will cause it anyway. They are not where they belong. It's as if you are carrying another human being on your back and they are constantly yelling in your ear about what they want. You might try to ignore it but it will influence you sooner or later to a greater or lesser degree.

These dear ones may get trapped in your physical form and not know how to get out. In such cases, a Divine Healing or other method of freeing these beings to enter into the Light must be done. In cases like these, a psychic surgery may be necessary to create something similar to a doorway for their exit as exhibited in the case of Renee and Mr. Jenkins, examined in detail later in this book.

The other types of entities requiring introduction are those classified as demonic in nature. These beings attach to, or live inside their hosts with the intention to do harm: for they thrive on suffering of all kinds. Some of them even have a mission. It is not an unknown concept to humanity that there has been a kind of spiritual warfare between Light and Darkness.

The demonic forces have their place and purpose, but it is not with you. It is not with humanity. It is no longer serving humanity to be in a polarized world where pain is the primary teacher. So these dealers of pain must now go and many are not willing to leave voluntarily. This is where the importance of Divine Healings truly surface, for angelic teams, including those with whom Wayne works: Jesus, Archangel Michael and Archangel Raphael, are able to remove them by force if necessary so that this world and the beings in it may ascend to a higher level of conscious awareness.

Another brand of entity that has not been specifically mentioned, are those that may be termed creatures. Some of these are demonic in nature and some are not inherently evil. They have many projected forms: from a tar-like sludge to multiple legged animal-like creatures and everything in between. These are conveniently included as a sub-category of the demonic entities previously discussed.

If you have an entity, your control has been compromised and this is one of the reasons you *mis-create*. This is an integral part of what stands between you and the glorious, joyful fulfillment of your dreams. God wants you to have a joyous experience on Earth. You did not come here—you were not born—to suffer. You are here to learn and to grow in joyous celebration!

Entities are not the only things that may directly interfere with your current quality of life and your advancement in this incarnation. There are also attachments. They can be fastened to one's physical body in an alternate dimension or plane, such as the spiritual plane or within the etheric or spiritual bodies. All of us have attachments, for a human being is made up of many layers; *you* are a very large being of Light.

There are many bodies that encircle your physical form—and they all have many layers. This creates a type of envelope around you, like an energetic onion and at the core of it is your physical form. There are many energy centers in your body called chakras. These energy centers have been compared to spinning plates and these plates overlap with the layers of our onion. Therefore, you have kind of a diced effect or grid that is formed around you. Attachments, both conscious and non-conscious, may lie in any of these grid squares. These are not confined to linear time and space; some are taking place in the distant past or future... right now.

Next, a brief explanation of the role of magic will assist you as you read the pages ahead. Magic can lie in any of these grid squares and in any of your body's physical, mental, emotional, spiritual and causal spheres. Not all magic is bad. Like all other things in the dimension of duality in which you live, there is a side that is of the Light and a side that is of the Darkness.

Black magic can indeed cause problems much like entities do. It can also be used in cooperation with entities. It is very dangerous. There are no friends in the darkness. There is no true benefit. The cost of its use is very high at the soul's level and can also be very high in the physical world. This writer, Arianna, has borne witness to one such outcome, where the deliberate user of black magic, a corroborator with dark entities suffered a terrible, crippling stroke that rendered him helpless when he was no longer fulfilling his side of the bargain.

The effects of black magic placement on the victim can result in many forms of sabotage. One that is important to address now is bindings. There is an example in this book of a man who was attacked with magic and bound energetically like a mummy; this allowed the entity that followed the black magic trail to enter his body.

Most of his experiences following this event were of constant struggle in numerous aspects of life. He was not free to expand in his life. Similar to a foot-binding in some cultures, the natural growth process of this man's life and spirit was severely stifled, resulting in a type of life deformity. Everything was painful and out of alignment. A Divine Healing can remove these types of restraints and help you to expand your life, allowing you to grow and realign that which has been stifled.

Bindings, while they may be imposed with something like energetic ropes, are not the same as cords. Cords have another purpose and are not necessarily magical but rather a naturally occurring phenomenon related to karma. They are an attachment that keeps one connected with a person, place or thing that occurred in the past, present or future.

If you have partnered with dark forces in past lives: entities, black magic, soul lessons in darkness; then they may still at this very moment be actively impacting your life. There is no shame in this, for it is the natural process. It is how your soul grows. It has indeed served a purpose but some of it no longer serves you and must be released for you to move into the next level of your evolution with ease and comfort.

Some of these attachments can cause problems. Sometimes they overshadow your efforts in a particular area of life or with particular people. Are there people in your life that always challenge you? Do not see these people as your enemies but rather as players in a show of your own creation. In the context of this explanatory chapter, we would say that some of these people are currently acting in a particular manner due to attachments you may have with them from other lifetimes.

Divine Healings are not limited to entity removal and cord cuttings. These healings are profound and deal with all of the layers of a human being: physical, emotional, mental and spiritual. Sometimes you are held back by wounds or by the holding of grief and negativity from your experiences in life. Carrying these deep-rooted negative emotions around in your heart, makes your heart an anchor that holds you back, that drowns you in despair.

Your heart is a profound, multidimensional energy center that has the ability to lead you right into heaven on Earth but it must be open for this to occur. A heart that is impacted with pain cannot open as easily and the dense negative energy will act as a block, a weight or a lock. Like a closet that is stuffed so full that you cannot open the door without being buried in hockey sticks and old Christmas decorations, you become afraid to open your heart because you have locked a giant mess inside that you fear will overtake you as a tidal wave of pain.

Jesus, Archangel Michael and Archangel Raphael can clear this pain-filled closet so that your heart's light may shine and lift you into a higher state of conscious being. Doesn't this sound wonderful? Imagine living your life with an *emotionally* new heart! Imagine starting a clean slate where the pains you felt and the burdens you carry no longer impact your life!

What is a Divine Healing? It is a direct connection with the higher Love of God. This is God's grace, God's mercy. All that is required for you to receive it is your willingness. Are you willing to receive the grace of God? Are you ready for your life to become the pure, creative experience you intended it to be when you began? Are you?

A healing of the kind that is witnessed and expressed in the following pages is done in partnership with Angels, God, and Jesus. The channeling healer is the conduit, or the bridge that allows this energy to be directed into a specific situation for each person. The Divine Healer is part of the physical aspect of a mostly non-physical team that makes it possible for this work to be completed. These healers are acting from a higher part of themselves when they are participating in this beautiful work. While the healer may not physically remove an entity from you, he or she will orchestrate those that have the capability.

Wayne, for example, works with Jesus Christ, Arch-angel Michael and Archangel Raphael. Each plays a different role in this work: Raphael and Michael work from the outside, coaxing, pushing and pulling entities out of the body. Sometimes the entities need to be removed surgically at the psychic level. Your physical body will not be harmed during a procedure like this but it will feel the effects of the absence of the entity that was taking up space inside. Much like recovering from physical surgery, you will need to rest, drink a lot of pure water and be kind and gentle with yourself.

Jesus helps with this process by working from the inside, pushing out all negativity with a powerful force of Love and Light until there is no room for entities and darkness. He fills the space—the void left by the absence so that where there was once darkness and negativity there could only be the Love and Light that is God; that is *you.*

After a Divine Healing or psychic surgery, it is common to experience a detoxification process for forty days. This is the process of your body releasing negativity and toxins at a safe and healthy rate after a healing of this nature. You may experience emotional symptoms, such as the need to cry or you may experience physical symptoms like feeling tired or rundown. You may even feel as if you're physically ill.

This is a temporary and necessary side-effect of the healing. If your body does not do this, you're healing will not be complete; it would be analogous to removing a cancerous growth but leaving behind all of the damaged cells it released into your body. Just like the removal of the malignant growth, this entity is gone forever but the negativity left behind can cause complications for your recovery.

Please do not misunderstand: there is work for you to do as well for a Divine Healing to have its highest, most beneficial expression through you. For whether you have been living under the influence of entities, magic, cords, past-life trauma or perverse energies like impacted negativity, you have become programmed to think, believe and act in certain ways. It is your responsibility and job to unravel this programming and mental conditioning.

You may be thinking that you have already tried this and it was too hard; the pull was too strong for you and you were swept out to sea. Once the spiritual and emotional aspects have been transformed, it is much easier to break free of the thinking and behaviors that you have manifested and you will be able to do it. A Divine Healing will even assist in the deprogramming process by activating synapses in your physical brain to help support your efforts. A Divine Healing is the true grace of God.

As you begin reading the remarkable stories of several individuals who have experienced the beautiful power of Divine Healings in the chapters that follow, you are encouraged to return to this chapter to refresh your memory regarding the definitions of any of these terms that are new or foreign to you.

MARIA

Growing up impoverished in the local public housing district was not easy for Maria—a butterfly, a delicate, bright splash of color—against the harsh, gray surroundings of her childhood. She endured extreme conditions: physical, sexual and emotional abuse that stripped her of innocence at a very young age. Maria was chided at school for being unkempt and because her shyness wouldn't allow her to smile at another person without covering her mouth; she was placed into Special Education.

"I used to hate life," she recounts. "And I used to pray to God since I was very young to help me, save me... and God never came."

After witnessing her brother receive a particularly vicious beating from their father, being punched in the face and then blown off by the local police who shared a special camaraderie with the assailant, Maria broke down.

"I remember that night, going into my room and telling God. 'If you're not gonna help me, maybe the Devil will.' And I felt like that night I called in the Devil to help me. I was so angry at God for what had just happened. My brother was hospitalized... I got beat, and I was begging for death... I couldn't take it anymore."

Later that night Maria had a bad dream wherein she witnessed a portal opening in the floor on the left side of her bed and she vividly remembers, "This nasty looking thing with green eyes came up." She screamed and ran from her room.

After that frightful night, Maria experienced a sudden, dramatic change in her personality. Everyone noticed that Maria became suddenly hard to ignore, wearing make-up and defending herself for the first time.

"I took control of my hair... over what I started wearing... and when girls picked on me, I would fight them back... I stopped being shy... I just started changing into this beauty... I was owning it." Attacks at school changed from, 'You smell, you're dirty, you have boogers!' to 'Who do you think you are? You're conceited.' When girls would push me in the hallway, I would always push them back... so from the sixth-grade on I had gotten into six or seven fistfights."

This was a drastic change because prior to the possession Maria would be frightened and back away from confrontation. When puberty hit and boys began to notice Maria, there was yet another metamorphosis in her demeanor. She created games to commandeer their attention and tallied kisses from over one-hundred boys when she was between the ages of twelve and fifteen.

She remembers this with mild amusement, "I used to like to make them cry for me, beg for me, gifts all the time. I was very much putting them through tests to declare their devotion to me."

These personality changes came on suddenly but were only subtle ripples on a moonlit lake compared to what dangerously manifested when Maria was fourteen. She had broken a house rule by taking her small dog, Mini, into the den with her to watch television. Her father had built this room and took great pride in it. Upon finding the two of them blissfully zoned-out, he burst through the entry—enraged, cursing.

"What the hell is that dog doing in here? I told you that the damn dog couldn't be in...."

He grabbed poor Mini and threw her violently down on the unforgiving floor. Quick to see that he was not done taking his anger out on the dog, Maria leapt courageously to the rescue, scooping Mini up into her arms and confronting her father for the first time. She found herself using violently abusive language and calling him names that are too vulgar to be printed here.

"Don't you ever hit her again... do you understand me? Don't you ever hit her again! You want to hit something? You hit me! You coward! You jerk! You hit me! C'mon, hit me! HIT ME! I hate you! Hit me!"

"You're a witch! Look at your eyes!" her father yelped, startled and pulling away from her.

Maria grabbed his shirt; a brazen move for a four-teen-year-old girl up against a large police officer with a boxing title.

"I am, and I'll kill you! Never hit me again! Do you understand me? You'll never hit me again! Never! Do you understand me? No man will ever do that to me again!"

Shaken and speechless, the abuser walked out of the room. He never hit Maria again.

Following this episode Maria found herself having frequent, angry outbursts over minor irritants such as being awakened prematurely from a nap, causing her siblings to nickname her the "Witch." She began suffering from anxiety attacks and was temporarily medicated with Valium that was too strong for her young body to process, leaving her groggy and disconnected. One night she felt a strong, unsubstantiated urge to pick up a pair of scissors and cut off all of her long, beautiful hair. In the following years, she would continue to feel suicidal and seek help from Jungian analysts, psychiatrists and psychologists but their talk therapy and medications proved perpetually ineffective.

Love making with Maria was like having two women at once: the first being sweet, gentle, open and loving and the second one making a screeching, venomous appearance only at orgasm.

Each time, Maria heard herself say, "Screw you! I hate you! Screw you!" to a man she had just made love with: and this appalled her deeply. An agitated voice in her head would say, "Let's get out of here. They should be paying you. Don't you give it away! They pay you for this!" Maria relates that the voice in her head, "Didn't like that they would have me—us—her—like that, taking us to that point."

Maria would always leave her partner's home immediately following one of these episodes and the relationship would end abruptly thereafter.

Maria met her husband when she was fifteen and they were married after a lengthy courtship. He was the only man that did not ignite the fury of the entity during intimate encounters. During the year 2002, Maria found a personal connection to the Divine that raised her into an ascended state, helping her to be a wonderful parent and thus kept the entity at bay. It seemed Maria had finally made it; she had it all: a handsome, loving husband, two beautiful children, a large, gorgeous home and a prestigious education... and a voice.

A voice that told Maria, "You're a bad person; you don't deserve this family. You're not good enough. Who do you think you are? Why did you say that? Are you that stupid?"

Maria's life became shrouded in shame; sometimes she didn't even feel worthy enough to get out of bed. Thoughts of suicide plagued her frequently.

Knowing the gentle embrace of the Divine made it all the more obvious to Maria that the violent tug that yanked her from the bosom of love was someone or something separate from herself. Men seemed to trigger the bizarre behavior most. Any time a male relative or her husband made even a remotely condescending statement, didn't take her seriously or tried to take a superior or dominant stance, Maria's personality would immediately and completely change.

One day she was having a discussion with her husband, who "wasn't hearing her." Standing in front of stacks of dishes and glasses on the kitchen countertops, Maria swept them all onto the floor, sending shards of broken glass everywhere. She found herself charging him—clawing at him—ripping his shirt off. He moved out after that and Maria's life was suddenly and utterly in ruin.

This was the last example of many appearances by the entity that Maria's husband endured and each time he would grab Maria, hold her down and snap his fingers saying, "Come back, come back, come back!" When she finally did he would tell her, "You were gone. It wasn't you. You were gone."

Maria lost her husband, her home, her prestigious socio-economic status and all that went with it. She grew reclusive, fearing that she could not control the savage thing within her that made her act in such violent, bizarre ways.

After her divorce, Maria's suicidal thoughts tormented her but a commitment to going within herself over the two years that followed proved enlightening and fruitful: this is when Maria came face-to-face with her inner demon. The angry, invading entity causing the disruption and destruction did not give a name, but she did share her story:

The entity was once a human in ancient Greece. She lived as a virgin and as a Channel (in Ancient Greece called an Oracle) for the priests of a temple dedicated to Apollo. She became a prisoner of the temple where she was required to obtain information through an indiscriminant, chemically induced trance-state that had many harsh repercussions on her physical body and emotional health. Her services brought in a great deal of money for the priests of the temple. When the Oracle could no longer perform her duties she was discarded: thrown into the street, penniless and alone. She was driven away by the rejection and abuse of local villagers and she cursed the priests who had committed this shameful act against her.

It became evident that when a scared, angry little eleven-year-old girl called out in the night, the Oracle thought "they were a good fit."

Maria learned that the Spirit Guides who seemed to share space with her and the entity were doing their best to perform damage control, keeping the raging, violent entity in a white room analogous to a padded cell but it wasn't enough. The displaced spirit would scream and throw herself around the room. She cut off almost all of her hair with a razor blade, leaving cuts and small bristly patches of hair sticking out of her scalp like mowed swamp grass. The entity had become an extremely ugly creature. Maria tells us of the new plan to stop the chaos this "being" was causing in her life.

"She, the entity, would start screaming in my head; throwing herself up against the wall... you know just throwing herself all over. She would drive me crazy and she was driving my Spirit Guides crazy! So one night they all made a decision... to kill her. They couldn't take her anymore. She used to wear a dirty, nasty white gown shredded at the bottom. Her head was shaved—she did it with a straight blade so it was cut—there were pieces: she'd become very ugly. She wanted me to cut my hair off too and I didn't do it."

Maria's guides told her, 'We have to kill her. We're going to hang her.' "I was there; I was participating. We get her out of the white room, we walk her and we hang her. I remember crying because I knew why she was the way she was. I knew she had suffered and suffered and suffered but... we had to kill her."

"The wise woman within me... she was just hugging me and saying 'We have to do it. You understand? We have to fly higher. We can't fly higher with her here. You are a vessel for Love and Light. She doesn't allow you... she's too dangerous... and she brings everybody down.' "

"So the entity was hanged but she didn't die! She kicked and screamed for a long time but then she just hung on the noose—alive but not moving—she didn't die... she stayed hung."

When Maria came to see Wayne for a session, it became evident to him that certain topics activated the disincarnate spirit who was with Maria and she would rage at Wayne at the most unexpected times: spewing tyrannical hatred when any topic that involved a male/female dynamic would arise.

Wayne recalls that, "Maria's voice changed. Her eyes changed."

The first time Wayne witnessed this he thought Maria was perhaps emotionally unstable. The second time, it became apparent to Wayne that it wasn't Maria who changed into a frenzied ball of hate towards men but *something inside Maria*. The third time was a test.

Wayne deliberately brought up a topic that he knew would set the entity off and when she emerged Wayne looked right into her eyes and said, "This is Wayne you're talking to!" and the fire left Maria's soulful brown eyes, immediately sweeping itself back into a hidden place.

It was in this moment that Maria realized: "*He sees her. He sees her! There's someone who can see her! There's someone who can help!*"

"What happened?" Wayne asked Maria, who was already in regret for what her unwanted partner had done.

"You scared it," she replied. "It's afraid of you."

Interestingly, Wayne didn't know what made him announce to the spirit who he was. He did not fully know at this juncture of his own spiritual discovery of the gift he carried and did not have any intellectual understanding that he could facilitate the removal of entities but he wanted to help Maria; she had suffered so much in the presence of this angry being she'd been carrying around with her since childhood.

Half-an-hour later, Maria was preparing to head off to her next appointment and as is customary in channeling circles, she and Wayne embraced to say goodbye. Wayne sensed that something was about to happen and felt influenced to glide Maria's arms to her side and give her a bear hug.

Pulling her up onto the balls of her feet, he found himself suddenly infused with a knowing of what to do. "Jesus, Michael, Raphael. I just kept saying it," Wayne recalls. "Jesus, Michael, Raphael. Jesus, Michael, Raphael."

Something was happening! Maria recounts her awareness in this moment of the purest energy of Love and Light she had ever experienced: she could feel the energy radiating from her feet.

"I knew something was different." Maria recalls, "I was so happy. So in love with everything, and life!"

Maria was flying so high, in fact, that she didn't even notice the massive blisters on the balls of her feet when she floated out of her session with Wayne.

She'd left the remarkable session in a cloud of love energy but within moments Wayne had awareness of the entity again... it was loose in the house! He could feel it—like a big gray blob—bouncing against his shielded auric field. Knowing angelic assistance was necessary Wayne called forth two angels and saw them escort this being into the heavens for healing and re-education. The entity could never return to haunt Maria or anyone else ever again; it was removed from this planet and dimension.

Wayne admitted that he had, "Learned a valuable lesson that day; you have to send them into the Light."

Since the entity removal the positive changes in Maria's life are evidence for her and her loved ones who cannot help but notice the new, more joyful Maria. Even her two young children have commented, "Mama, you're more happy."

Maria has far less anger than before and no more hateful tirades. She is more patient and forgiving. She's no longer a recluse, procuring many friends and a stable relationship that is no longer about being served by her partner but about having an affectionate, mutual exchange of love and companionship. She has taken several channeling classes and has surpassed her previous levels of ascension.

Maria's third sight (sometimes called the third eye) has opened up even more, allowing her to see the invisible, conscious entities and burdens carried by others that she can now help! It has been revealed to her that she has been called to compassionately help disincarnated spirits who are latched onto others return to where they belong: the Light. Gently and lovingly she coaxes them into their next phase of evolution where they cannot return to those they previously inflicted with their own hang-ups, emotional issues or agendas.

In Maria's words:

"Everyone has noticed a change in me: my mother, my father, my children, my ex-husband, my closest friends have noticed... I've changed for the better. Calmer, not so anxious, not so nervous, not so scared... not so angry and being able to really open to love with a man."

RENEE

Renee was a rambunctious child raised in a religious Christian family with a long line of psychics and other gifted ancestors in her family's history. Beginning at a very young age, Renee felt that there was more to life than what she had been told and she intended to find out what it was that went beyond the fact that she "was brought up to know, to see, to feel what's going on." She was prepared to uncover, to discover the truth, with or without guidance from her parents.

It has been said that idle minds are the Devil's playground and one afternoon twelve-year-old Renee and her eight-year-old sister, Jackie, decided to test the boundaries of what they'd been taught. By experimenting with the Ouija Board, a tool for contacting the spirit realm and marketed as a harmless game, they called in an entity whose identity was revealed many years later as Mr. Jenkins.

Through the planchette skimming the board beneath their fingers, Mr. Jenkins kept spelling out a name: J-A-C-K-I-E. He was asking for her, and questions about her, for example, "What were Jackie's desires?"

Renee was highly disturbed by the narrow interest in her innocent little sister and asked Jackie to leave the room. When she did, the Ouija Board flew violently out of Renee's hands and landed abruptly across the room. The angry entity was loose in the house.

The entire family noticed strange things happening around the house after this incident. In addition to a marked increase in conflict and chaos within the household there were also many of the typical signs of spirit intrusion: doors opening by themselves, beds shaking in the dark and televisions turning on-and-off without prompting. Renee remembers a distinct sense of being followed by something evil.

Mr. Jenkins was not content to just cause discord and spooky mischief around the house; he wanted some-one to latch on to—a partner, one that was willing... or not. As related frequently in other cases beyond this book, the entity made its move while Renee slept, while she was dreaming of a sleepover with friends.

"That night when I went to bed I went into this really deep sleep and I had a dream that all my friends came over for a slumber party. We were just having a good time in my room: my boyfriend, best friend, a couple other friends and my sister... then they all went to the kitchen and I was just laying there and I was waiting for them to come back... and my hand was hanging over the side of the bed and I felt something brush my arm! I looked over to the side and as soon as I did I saw this short being with pointy ears and very black hair and the eyes were white with no pupils, nothing—and he just jumped up and started choking me... when he did that I was physically choking while still asleep!"

"When this occurred I knew I was in my dream... I was locked into my dream and I was in between a dream and an awakened state and I said 'I plead the blood of Jesus Christ!' "

At the exact moment of her plea, Renee sat straight up in her bed and Jackie did too.

"I can't breathe! I can't breathe! Oh my God!" Renee panted between gulps of air.

The girls could hear their father racing through the house toward their room and he quickly burst through the door with the hope of receiving an explanation as to what caused him to awaken so abruptly, so panic-stricken from a sound sleep. Renee's father was a very religious man and she did not want to cause further disruption or division within her family by describing everything.

So she said, "I don't know what happened. I don't know. Something crazy happened. I, I don't know!" But what she knew to be true was, "I had allowed him to come in, because I wasn't as strong as I thought I was, because I was young."

Renee's mother knew of spirits and could sense the presence of Mr. Jenkins. Renee's new unruliness and bitterness convinced her mother that she had been possessed by the entity. Renee's mother arranged for an exorcism for her daughter and home. This yielded little result but Renee believed that she could control the entity even if she could not evict him.

Mr. Jenkins continued to inflict harm within Renee's inner world by imposing nasty words and evil thoughts into a mind that did not generate such things before the possession. He would swoop in like a black cloud, take shape and hold her down so that she was physically restrained.

According to Renee, he would say abusive things like, " 'You're ugly, you're stupid,' and degrading stuff like that. It makes you think evil thoughts... sometimes you'll think, 'I could actually feel bad at this moment. What would happen if I... killed that person?' You just start thinking crazy things that you would never, ever think about."

"It's made a lot of bad decisions for me in my life. It made me take on karmic duties that I didn't have to take on... like taking care of people, hindering my personal progress. It's like you're swimming to a finish line but you're dragging a brick with you and you can't finish... and you're so frustrated because you don't know what's hindering you. But you know what you're thinking and you know what you want, but something's stopping you."

"There were a lot of things I knew I needed to do in my life—spiritually—and I couldn't do them because it made me believe that I didn't have the power to." One of those things was channeling, which Renee felt blocked from learning.

It is unknown whether or not it was Mr. Jenkins' influence that led Renee to get involved with a handsome young man who became her live-in partner. He was diagnosed with cancer and she became his primary caregiver. Renee soon realized that there was another presence within her boyfriend in addition to the cancer that was contributing to his sadness, depression and frustration. She felt it and it paid *her* personal visits when the blanket of despair that permeated the house fell over her like a collapsing canopy.

"That one was a real dark entity and when it came in it would strap me down where I couldn't speak, or get up: basically, I'd be paralyzed. I have really been conscious of it since I was with my ex-boyfriend, which was about seven years ago. I have a feeling that it was from him because he was surviving cancer and there was so much sorrow, so much... there was a lot of negativity that would come into our home."

"I would chant, and I would dust (spiritually cleanse) the house. When he was sleeping I would bless him and that spirit would get angry... and the house would be clean for a while and then it would come back again. My ex and I have a spiritual connection. He knows what I'm talking about when we visit, or talk on the phone. He'll say, 'The spirit, the spirit came,' you know? And when he gets attacked, he calls me immediately and tells me what happened. To me it feels like it was just interfacing with my own de-mons. I don't know."

When Renee was thirty-seven, a close childhood friend had a successful entity removal and healing from Wayne and his beloved Spirit Guides and suggested that she might benefit from such a session too. Renee relates a slew of seemingly random diffi-culties on the morning of her appointment with Wayne.

"As soon as I made the call to Wayne I started to get a pain on my left side. When I was done with the phone call I tried to get up out of my bed and I fell down because the pain was so excruciating... as soon as I got up the whole bottom part of my body felt like it was gonna fall out. That entity was scared. It wanted me to stay home... he didn't want to be revealed but I was getting ready and I was fighting the pain. And it would get stronger and stronger when I was making the decision that I better just go. I felt like I was gonna throw up... I knew what was happening. I knew something was trying to keep me from going."

"I got in my van and the gas gauge was on empty. It was not on empty the night before! And I hit every light you could think of—every traffic thing you can think of—there was construction everywhere. It was remarkable... and all I could do was just laugh because I knew what was going on!"

After arriving at her appointment, Wayne explained to Renee that physical discomfort or illness was common when Archangel Raphael "starts pulling the entities in." He described how the process and session might evolve because the structure is often the same. After a prayer inviting in all of the highest, best and most helpful parties, especially Jesus, Archangel Michael, and Archangel Raphael, Wayne enters into a channeled state and the healing begins.

Raphael acts as the spokesperson but Wayne can sense the other members of the team standing-by, ready to do whatever is necessary to safely, completely and permanently return the intruding entities to the Light. Through a loving and gentle but very high frequency, Archangel Raphael began preparing Renee's body for the psychic surgery she was soon to experience. This is very different than physical surgery since the body itself receives no wound but the ethereal body is opened for the purpose of removing an entity or another form of perverse energy. This is not always necessary but it was in Renee's case.

Raphael asked that the entities that were invading Renee's body and world go peacefully and voluntarily, or they would be removed against their will. Mr. Jenkins, who was four-feet tall, was willing to go with the angels off of this planet to be healed. However, he was so large that they had to create a psychic incision from Renee's left armpit to her left hip so he could get out. Archangel Michael took the entity's hand and escorted him out of Renee and into the Light so that he could never return to the planet to invade and harm another soul.

The second entity was not so reasonable. And Jesus entered Renee's body to flood the entity out with Love and Light while Raphael pushed it from one side, and Michael pulled it out of her like a rope of despair. This entity was also removed from the planet to prevent harm to others.

It did not take the team long to do the entire procedure and when they were finished, both entities were gone forever. They were completely removed, not only from Renee but from the planet: and are never able to return. The healings performed by this Divine Team are absolute and permanent.

Raphael directed Renee to obtain a copy of Betsy-Morgan Coffman's *Protection and Cleansing CD* to prevent future vulnerability because it is not unusual for a spiritual person to attract dark entities like moths to a flame. She was also advised how to ease the physical and emotional after-effects of a healing of this magnitude since she would continue to cleanse and heal for the next month.

Renee's body was sore for two weeks and then she went through a period of cyclic physical illnesses that continued to cleanse her body. This was necessary to remove the remaining negativity and residue left over from the long-term residence of the previous, destructive entities.

Once on the other side of her cleansing process, Renee was free to begin noticing the changes in her life. Immediately following the session Renee was able to see her long-time friend, another client of Wayne's, who noted immediately that Renee "was glowing again."

There have been many exciting changes in Renee's inner and outer worlds since her meeting with Wayne. Within months of the healing, Renee found the will and resources to fulfill her long-term dream of opening a boutique. This flourishing business also has an Internet presence that markets a variety of handmade art, jewelry and crafts.

Unhealthy long-term behaviors that Renee felt influenced to engage in have since ceased completely, including an insatiable drive to constantly seek out the attention of men. She has lost weight and placed healthy boundaries on her relationships with ex-lovers and anyone who would drain her energy. She has reconnected with her high school sweetheart after twenty years of separation, finding that their love is still vibrant and alive, but she is now able to receive it in a way that she was unable to before. They are engaged and planning to marry this year.

The most profound effect the healing has had in Renee's life is that it has given her a sense of peacefulness she had never experienced. She is also "more clear minded, focused and spiritually in tune." She feels healthier, wiser, well grounded and much more positive: and this has been reflected back to her in the form of success.

ARIANNA

I remember my early childhood as a joyful and magical phenomenon. I knew who I was, and I spoke to the plants and trees in the late afternoon while the sun graced us in its warm embrace through the quivering leaves in the summer's gentle breezes. All my needs were met and I knew God through many means; as the angels encased me in his all-knowing, unconditional, loving embrace. There was nothing I feared to be beyond the touch of the Divine.

It wasn't until my pre-teen years that shadow crept into my world like swollen cloud cover; taking the form of a variety of neuroses and mental malfunctions labeled over the years as: Obsessive Compulsive Disorder (OCD), Bi-polar Disorder, acute depressive episodes and Attention Deficit Disorder (ADD).

In my memory, I was fine one day and crazy the next. Once, I was with my grandmother in the car when I suddenly had the feeling that my hands were dirty. At twelve-years-old I looked at them: my palms, the smooth skin on top, even under my fingernails and there was nothing visible to the naked eye. Still, I couldn't shake the thought and it expanded in my mind until I could think of nothing else but washing them... just to make sure. But I was never sure; I lost the ability to trust my own perceptions in what seemed like an instant and I spent the next several years trying to wash the skin off of my hands and body to purify myself... but I never felt cleansed.

The visits with psychologists, psychiatrists, social workers and family doctors proved largely fruitless. Even the strong doses of various, ever-changing medications, behavioral exercises and talk therapy sessions gave little positive result: I was essentially told that I had to learn to live with my paranoia, depression and isolation to the best of my ability. I felt completely out-of-control, completely powerless; and I am not sure that the professionals hired for my benefit felt much differently!

During eighth and ninth-grade, I had to be home-schooled because I perceived danger everywhere. I often thought that I saw contaminates in unusual places, like the counter at the lunch-line or on the ceiling of the band room at school. I was afraid of human contact and gradually surrendered to my isolation and terror.

OCD was only the entrance to a long, dark staircase with no railings that I followed deep into a realm of misery that cascaded into more misery, more pain, more suffering, more isolation: and greater mad-ness's, including a compulsive need to cut myself.

Although I didn't realize it while in the midst of the mental carnage, this behavior was an attempt to cleanse the darkness that was consuming me. I carried these manifestations with me for seventeen years.... Seventeen years of going into deep depressive states where I often fantasized about my own death—a sweet release, I thought—for a person with no intrinsic worth or value.

In response to my own thoughts and beliefs about myself, the Universe delivered to me others who carried energies like my own and the damaged, bleak souls that came and went from my life reinforced my understanding that I was unworthy of love; that there was no good in the world set aside for me.

My behaviors made no sense. I was drawn to dance on the edge of death as often as possible; frequently taking inappropriate risks with my health, life and safety. I turned to drugs and alcohol for relief, which only deepened the problem. I was afraid of people—I couldn't relate and didn't know how to be socially appropriate. I found myself actually searching for abusive relationships. I was fearful all the time. *All the time.* In a constant state of terror there is no reason, no logic and no basic sanity.

Love dropped away from my world and all that was left were cold shadows and the deceitful faces of others who hid under lying masks, just like me. We consistently and repeatedly fooled each other. And at the end of each episode, there was always that temptation to end it all... I will never forget the day that I was racing head-on to meet a telephone pole in my crummy jalopy, thinking that I could make the pain stop once and for.... It was only the grace of God that influenced me to turn the wheel sharply at the last second, yanking me dramatically from the dripping fangs of death.

After sixteen years of turmoil and trauma, I found myself to be the full-time caregiver and legal guardian of a man who was more than twice my age of twenty-three when we met. Our relationship was a union made in darkness and while he had a reasonable understanding of what that meant, I did not.

We moved from New York to New Mexico several years into our relationship. Approximately one year later he suffered a terrible stroke that left him severely crippled—without the ability to communicate effectively. His anger, misery and fear mingled with mine and my world shrank to the size of a mustard seed.

During that year of brooding and mourning everything became gray, as if the entire house had been coated in ash or soot. This feeling was not completely foreign to me because I had experienced it off and on for most of my life. Mercifully, there was a knowing someplace deep within me that there was color in the world, somewhere. Other people saw brilliant, deep pools of blue, soothing shades of lavender, fierce pinks and vibrant greens. I envied them and wanted to rejoin this world of Light, so I made one decision and it was this: *I will do one thing that I have never done before.*

It never occurred to me that such a simple decision, a non-committal choice would lead me back into the arms of goodness and grace, or that the journey would be so transformative and miraculous. I chose to attend a local channeling group in Albuquerque that I'd discovered on the Internet.

I didn't know what channeling was; I only knew of its supernatural connotations. I was expecting to walk into a dark, candlelit room with a woman leaning over a crystal ball waiting for the table to move, or for a glass to mysteriously come flying across the kitchen, but instead, I was met by a loving group of people who gathered there to listen to "Spirit" speak messages of Love for them through the hostess, who was also the Channel.

I found channeling to be mysterious and uplifting. I began to attend sessions weekly and became a quick believer in this amazing phenomenon. I found myself smiling, even in the face of tremendous despair. I sang. I even began the process of weaning myself from the medications that I had been taught to rely upon for glimpses of sanity. I thought it must be an amazing advantage to be able to communicate in a two-way format with loving spirits from the higher realms and decided that I wanted to learn this art form myself, so I took a class.

As promised, I did indeed "channel" before my Level-One Class was completed but I was experiencing a lot of physical pain when I practiced at home so I drew back from the art form until I was able to take the Level-Two Class, which deepens the student's connection to the higher dimensional beings I was trying to communicate with.

We discovered that my ill, live-in partner had energetically wrapped himself around my heart and it was causing a variety of problems including physical pain, as well as a sensation that my chest was being squeezed or sat upon for unnaturally long periods of time.

I continued to meet weekly with my channeling group and felt that my inner world was beginning to change. Even in the face of the despair that I continued to spend most of my time within, there was a glimmering sliver of light that I looked at ceaselessly and it was becoming increasingly effective for protecting me from the crumbling emotional rubble all around my natural environment.

It was within this group that I met Wayne; who would share with me the experience of a professional, Level-Three Class (C-3) in the coming months. My own gifts were beginning to emerge and I was getting a lot of information through my third eye chakra. This is the energy center located just above and between the eyes on the human body and it is where predictions and visions are most often received. In addition to learning about the business-end of being a professional psychic, C-3 required us to complete at least three readings per week for others but there was nothing I looked forward to more than our group coming together to channel for each other.

The loving spirits that came through each member of the group helped us to form surprisingly deep connections with each other over a relatively short period of time and Wayne's primary channeling guide, Archangel Raphael, had many loving messages for me regarding my situation at home, my partner's health and my own inner struggles.

I had also been getting sick frequently for many months with a serious pneumonia-like condition that the doctors could not keep at bay. I knew the seriousness of this issue because I had gone to an Urgent

Care Clinic more than once... I was feeling quite frightened that my lungs were going to shut down and I beseeched Raphael for guidance and healing. I was told that my home life was affecting my health and getting out of that situation was the key to my well being. *Then I saw it.*

About halfway through C-3 and a couple of days before one of our meetings: it made its first appearance. I couldn't see much of it—just its hideous snout—its sharp teeth—an abandoned special-effect from a Hollywood set... emerging from my sore, wheezing chest! By this time I was accustomed to receiving visions but this one was so bizarre and I had no idea what it could possibly be. No one had spoken of anything other than warm, fuzzy, Love and Light. Where did visions like this fit into all of that?

In the days that followed it appeared more often and more fully. It was neckless, like a giant brown worm with a vicious temper; predatorial and deranged. I wondered if it was the truth about what I had become: a result of being a part of so much ugliness during my lifetime.

Its repeated appearances were increasingly disturbing so I asked about it at the next C-3. A loving energy came through the Channel and explained that this vision was indeed real, and furthermore, it was not a part of me. It was alien—an energy that embodied the pain and suffering I had been experiencing *since twelve-years-old!*

It could be removed, I was told, in more than one fashion but that the fastest way to eliminate its presence was to have a healer "like Wayne" evict it. I was told that this creature was indeed anchored within my body and it resided in my lungs and throat area; it was linked to my persistent pneumonia! Wayne sat next to me quietly as I wondered if he would help.

We always closed channeling classes by holding hands in a circle while our teacher prayed. That evening I didn't hear one word because when Wayne took my hand my attention was immediately drawn to the surge of energy that seemed to originate with him. This burst of energy traveled up my arm and into my chest cavity where the creature was anchored in my physical form. That's when I heard its voice for the first time. Well, it wasn't a voice, really—more like a berserk, high-pitched scream and I watched from my third eye as the monster writhed in pain... as if it was being electrocuted.

I saw that it had arms: tiny and inhuman—cartoonish—comically disproportionate to its apparent body size. The monster became quiet when Wayne released my hand and I asked him if he would help me. He humbly agreed to try and an appointment was made several days in advance.

It was a long, dark ride home that night because the perverse creature I had discovered had an intelligent consciousness of its own: it did not wish to come in contact with Wayne and his guides again. *It had an actual agenda!* It intended to frighten me away from anyone or anything that had the power to evict it from my body, as its host.

As I was driving home it came out of my chest cavity farther than it ever had before—snakelike—and twisted itself around to face me. We were face-to-face. It roared. It showed me its rows of razor-sharp teeth, dripping with saliva—a warning—it was not going to go easily.

Instead of being frightened, I found myself indignant—angry at the beast—it had robbed me! It had stolen my childhood, my joy, my sense of self-love, self-worth... and I wanted it out. I yelled at it—cursing—swearing that it would be banished from me if it was the last thing I was ever to do. It retreated back into my body, curling up like the world's ugliest brooding cat.

I had been anxiously looking forward to my appointment with Wayne but when I pulled up to his home, the hideous beast was still taunting me, staring at me through conscious eyes of blackness—pools of ink—threatening and unsettling. I no longer wanted to be controlled by this entity and my fear had now transformed into a hopeful determination to be freed from the creature forever. I realized that I was about to get an opportunity to find out who I really am... maybe I was a happy person underneath all of the puppeteering this malevolent entity had been interjecting for so many years.

Maybe the root cause of my seemingly endless depression, confusion and string of traumatic incidences wasn't what I had been previously led to believe. Maybe it wasn't hopeless; maybe there were good things in store for me and they were only being blocked by *this thing—this thing* that had been feeding on my despair like lemon drops for most of my life. Maybe....

I felt comfortable with Wayne and Archangel Raphael right away and knew that there was finally hope for me. I explained what I had been seeing and experiencing and then I was asked to sit facing-away from Wayne for the healing. Neither one of us seemed to know exactly what to expect but after a beautiful prayer for protection and the highest, best guides and angels available for this healing: and a specific invitation extended to John the Baptist, Jesus Christ, Archangel Raphael and Archangel Michael... the battle began.

Wayne placed his left hand on my back and his right hand on my arm and within seconds I felt the energy lock into me; Wayne's hand was pulled against my back like it was magnetically attracted and I felt an energetic battle raging within my physical body and all around me. My body writhed and jerked around— the entity refused to depart. It was not willing to go; it had fed on my misery for many years and had no intention of leaving without a fight.

In my case, the entity had to be forcibly removed by those who have become fondly known to me as *my favorite team*: Jesus, Michael, and Raphael. Jesus entered into my body to address the darkness from the inside-out, Archangel Raphael and Archangel Michael pushed and pulled this entity out of my body, my energy field and off this planet.

Jesus filled the great void with more Love and Light than I could hold and I left there feeling as if I'd shed thirty pounds; I was practically floating. I had a sense of joy and peace unlike any I have ever experienced. I knew intuitively that my life had just been permanently changed in the most benevolent way.

I was instructed to continuously fill myself with Love and Light over the next forty-eight hours and drink as much water as possible to help flush out any toxins that were released inside my body when the entity was removed. After all, there were tons of negativity that had to be dispersed and cleansed.

I was told that my life was about to make a 180-degree turn now that I was no longer under the control of darkness, but that the conditioning I had experienced from all the years of negative influence was my own work to undo. I was to guard my thoughts and begin telling a new story—a happy, joyful tale of who I am now—a story that embraced and embodied all that I ever desired for myself.

I spent the rest of that miraculous day of grace pampering myself guiltlessly. Later that evening I joined a tele-group of people planning to experience the ascension energies of Orion, a star-being and teacher-guide with whom I was familiar. It was his frequency that connected me to the higher realms at the beginning of this amazing spiritual renaissance and I still call upon him often.

In the ascension energies I actually saw Jesus, and beside him in a cage on the "ground" that we stood upon was the creature. The message was clear: *it can never come back.* Jesus stood adjacent to me and blasted a powerful stream of Light into my spiritual body, and as he did, beloved Archangels' Michael and Raphael joined us. *I was free! I am free!*

When I saw Jesus I also saw myself, as if I was standing just outside the scene and watching it take place. These visions and spiritual experiences are unique to each person. When I saw Jesus it was very clear to me that it was him but my visions are usually not as defined as third dimensional sight.

Since this nasty creature has been removed from my body, mind and soul—never to return—my world has blossomed in ways I could never have predicted. I have remained off *all* of my Bi-polar, OCD and ADD medications as I continue plowing ahead as a Warrior of Light.

The pursuit of channeling has become my greatest joy. I have become a very clear, accurate Channel for Love: it has continued to expand upon itself; bringing more love, laughter, joy and peace into my life—even in the midst of impossible circumstances. Learning to teach others how to channel is another delight that I have experienced and I have founded a channeling group that holds a variety of channeled workshops on topics of interest in this arena.

I have learned that things are not always as they seem... that I have many gifts that have been either dormant or misunderstood. These gifts have opened like the petals of a lotus and bring me tremendous fulfillment as I am directed to use them for the highest good of myself and others. The wreckage that I attracted into my life now smolders in the distance: I am moving on to my higher purpose of joyously creating within the Love and Light of God.

My guides have been helping me to continue healing and have begun the process of working through me to heal others. I have recently been joined by my old friends: Jesus, Michael and Raphael, to offer to others on appropriate occasions, what had been offered to me through Wayne. I am learning to live in a channeled state that offers me various timeframes of living from a higher perspective: Love.

I used to be a very selfish person, with thoughts primarily about myself, but now I feel an unquenchable desire to reach out and lend a hand to those who might want to take it. And even those who don't because from a place deep within me I want everyone to experience the love and joy of God.

I envision more miracles and an opportunity to bring Light to dark places that I never dreamed possible. For me, this is a complete turn-around from the misery I endured before channeling, Jesus, the Angels and Wayne came into my life. I am in love with living again and I see my future as a bright, glistening star of abundance, joy and love.

KAREN

Karen suffered from sleep paralysis for as long as she could remember. Victims of this phenomenon have complained throughout history of the sensation that something is pushing on their chest and/or reaching down their throat; accompanied by hallucinatory and frightful images of a variety of unfriendly beings. Karen's chilling description of the experience is expressed below for the readers' understanding of this occurrence that has been reported throughout the ages.

"What happens is... at some point in your sleep, you wake up and you're conscious but you can't move. If you wake up in a sleep paralysis episode you're completely conscious and you go out of your body. You can see the room that you're in, and you can see yourself... it's a terrifying experience. It's not a pleasant out-of-body experience; it's a feeling of entrapment because even though you're lucid and conscious you can't move! And then you start having hallucinations. It would be a dream but because you're awake it's more like a hallucination... or maybe it's not a hallucination. You start seeing things in the room. Since I was a kid, I've had three shadowy figures that stand around me."

"Sometimes they'll sit on the end of the bed and they'll crawl up onto my chest just like the classic depictions... and they'll push down on my chest and they'll stick their hand—it's like an invisible hand—that goes right down your throat and you'll think they're gonna choke you! You go into a panic because... you don't make the distinction that this is happening on a psychic level and it's not happening on a physical level... you think everything is literal... but actually, no harm has ever come to my physical body from it."

"They've done lots of different things to communicate with me. One thing they've done is communicated... through some sort of information transmission through my mind (telepathy) and I don't know what they're telling me, but I know it doesn't feel good. Sometimes they take information from me. It's sort of like you're paralyzed and someone's doing some kind of surgery that you didn't give consent for... sometimes they'll dress up as a family member and trick me into thinking I'm awake and interacting with someone. I wake up in a dream, my body is paralyzed but I start hallucinating that my daughter has come into the room and she's talking to me, but she won't show me her whole face. She's got half of her face turned and one eye looking at me, and she's going 'Mommy...' and I'm saying, 'Show me your face. Show me your face,' and then it's a demon."

Karen suffered through these episodes from as few as six times per year to as many as six times per month. Triggers seemed to depend on a variety of factors ranging from stress to a simple disruption or change in her sleeping pattern.

Becoming a channeling student of Betsy-Morgan Coffman was the beginning of relief for Karen. In her Level-Two Channeling Class she had an opportunity to ask another student a question about her sleep paralysis episodes and received a startling confirmation of her suspicions.

According to her fellow student, "Well, they're demons. They're from a past life and they want to pull you back. They're trying to pull you back. They're attached to you and they're following you, and they want to influence you. They're attracted to your light and they want to pull you back into the darkness."

Betsy suggested to Karen that she should make an appointment with Wayne to get to the bottom of the matter and have it resolved. Inexplicably, Karen didn't contact Wayne until she was well-immersed in her Level-Three Channeling Class (C-3). When she told Wayne of her episodes, he explained that he had never heard of the disorder and scheduled an appointment with her a week or two in advance.

Karen continued to describe the events before her appointment with Wayne, "The week before that... they must have known that they were on their way out... because I was like a battlefield that week. I was going through horrible feelings of resentment, irritability—I actually punched somebody. I was so angry— just toxic—oozing and tired, and I was low."

"Someone would make a mistake and I'd get furious with them, for the simplest mistake, like they spilled milk. The funny thing about it was I knew every time that emotion would come up and those behaviors would come out, I'd have this awareness of, '*What are you doing?*' Like there was another part of me that was going, '*You know that that's not a big deal, that what they did is okay, that they're human... look at yourself: you're riddled with mistakes and with flaws... what are you doing?*' But the feeling of anger and judgment and hostility towards others and lack of tolerance was so much more powerful... which made me feel really bad about myself. I really felt like I couldn't fight the good fight, and then I continued to blame other people and really could not see my own error... in the moment. Where the anger was coming from I didn't even know; I couldn't get to the bottom of it."

"I was trying to ascend and go into the Light and transform and at the same time I was being pulled back by... habituated behaviors that I couldn't repro-gram because I was under the control of something else... I was being fed Light through education, channeling, and all these wonderful experiences, and I knew that I wanted to go forward and I wanted to change and not be that person anymore, but I couldn't do it! There was this horrible sense of pow-erlessness, '*Why don't I have control over my behav-ior?*' I couldn't stop myself... from acting out or being mean or vicious if I'd push people away. I'd have to just sit in my room and be alone and be irritable and go, '*Why can't I get rid of this feeling?*' "

It was during a C-3 meeting that all of her conflicting energies and thoughts seemed to come together as one overwhelming tidal wave for Karen. She remem-bers that many of the messages she received from other channeling students in the class were that she did not love herself. This did not match her perception of her personality and became a source of frustration for her throughout the six-week class.

"Betsy had an assignment: bring three books that you want to use to support your learning as a Channel. I brought my three books and I was introducing them to the group... then I told a joke. I said, 'Here's my three books that I'm not gonna read!' I just don't have the time. To me, it's humorously self-aware but I'm learning that to other people it looks like I'm putting myself down. That's just who I am; I'm loose and I make fun of myself and it's my way of lightening up. So I made this joke and everybody runs it through this Karen-doesn't-love-herself-filter."

"Someone in the class said, 'If we had a quarter for every time you put yourself down....' That was the last straw. When she said that, all of the other messages and feedback and all the feelings of misunderstanding that have been inside me... something just snapped and I felt that I couldn't hold back anymore!"

Karen's mind was spinning in a tornado of frustration and anger, "'Stop telling me that I don't love myself! Stop telling me I put myself down! Stop telling me that my self-love isn't there because it is and you're not getting me, you're not seeing me!' I stopped listening to the group after she said that; I was in a little Karen box. And I was thinking, 'You don't get me. Stop saying that! You don't see me. You don't see me. They don't see you. You are big and beautiful and bright, and you do love yourself and you do know who you are and they're telling you that you *don't!*' It was this strange... a lot of it was coming from the Light and part of it was coming from the ego, going, '*They don't believe you've got it. You can't prove it to them.*' "

As Karen churned in her own internal juices for a lifetime of perceiving being unseen and unheard for her authentic self, she began to feel pain in the area of her solar plexus, "Like a knife went right into me. I suppose it's more like a knife came right out of me, because it came from the inside and it hurt really bad. I was seeing that the pain I was experiencing in my body was completely related to the thoughts I was having in my mind. I didn't know how intense it was going to get though, so I just started breathing deep. I was trying to be appropriate."

"I realized within about one minute that it wasn't gonna stop and that something was happening. I looked at my friend, who was sitting across from me and I just stared at her until I got her attention, and she looked at me and she goes, 'Are you okay?' And I mouthed the words, '***Help me!***' "

"And my friend said, 'What's wrong?' When she said that, everyone looked at me and Betsy said, 'Oh my gosh! Are you okay? Do you want to get in the middle of the circle?' They must have seen it on my face. I looked at Betsy, and... my heart cracked open and I felt all the pain of my whole life... feeling every moment that I've ever felt misunderstood or not seen for who I really was."

At this point, Karen had been experiencing physical pain for less than three minutes but as she entered the center of the circle of loving friends wishing to heal her, the physical and emotional pain became one, "That's when it got really, really intense because I couldn't differentiate what was happening in my heart, and what was happening psychologically, and what was happening in my body—it was all one."

She recalls a feeling of being ripped open, "I just started crying really hard and I said, 'It hurts! It hurts! It hurts!' It really felt sharp—it was like something was growing. It felt like it was very localized in the solar plexus and I felt like I wanted to have an outpouring of grief and pain. I wanted to purge it. Everyone—so loving—they immediately put their hands around me and start sending me Light. Betsy gets on her knees right in front of me and she starts praying for Light, angels, support and assistance and then she told it to leave."

The pain increased in intensity; Karen found herself on her knees, rocking back-and-forth and bawling into her hands. Richard, a friend of Betsy's and a healer she'd known for many years, was present that evening and he suggested that Karen lie down.

As she did, "He put his hands over the pain and it was so helpful because I immediately felt the Light go in." Karen recalls, "It really helped with the physical pain. Every time he'd lift his hand up I would grab it and bring it back there because if he just moved his hand a little bit the pain was right underneath it."

When the pain started to move away from under Richard's hands and move from any place where there was someone sending in Light, it became apparent that it was no ordinary physical or psychological ailment.

"It started moving to other parts of my body... like a mouse being chased out of a house. At one point it split into two and it was on either side of my abdomen. At another point it went into my head, but someone put their hand there and it dropped back down into my gut. It seemed like it was a real gut-oriented entity—that that was its home."

"They say that the liver is associated with anger; and that's probably where it was living because that's where I was feeling it. It just hurt so bad and at some point I became aware that there was going to be an entity removal—that there was something inside of me that needed to be taken out. I knew there was something inside of me."

While Karen was doing her best to bring in, and let in as much Light as possible, there was an opposing force within her that impressed thoughts upon her mind such as, " 'You're faking it. You're putting on a show. You're a drama queen. Cut it out! You just want attention. This isn't really happening. You're stupid. You're wasting people's time. They're trying to help you. It's getting so late at night right now. People wanted to go home. You're just wasting their time. Look at you. Look at how selfish you are.' "

"It wanted me to go into denial so that I wouldn't let it out but then there was this profound Light experience on the battlefield that's going, *I want to be healed! Let me go! I want God!*' It was really like when people say you've got a Devil and an Angel—it was just like that—that whole dichotomy, and here I am in the middle of it."

"At the same time, I became aware of things in my life that needed to heal. All of a sudden, I go, 'Could somebody please send love to my mother?' and I started crying, 'I don't love my mother enough.' A lot of strange things came out of my mouth. I remember asking, 'Betsy, am I gonna be okay after this? I want a good life.' I started answering to the doubts inside of me. *'I want a good life. I want to be healed. I want to go forward. I want to do service. I want to serve the Light. This is my path! I want to love my mother. I want to be more grateful. This is who I really am!'* "

After about an hour of energy work from the group with little, sustained improvement, Betsy decided it was time to call Wayne. He arrived within fifteen minutes and after seeing the severity of Karen's condition, he got to work right away, calling in protection, Light, 100,000 angels, and of course Jesus, Archangel Michael and Archangel Raphael.

"Wayne comes in and everyone just sort of moves back. After sitting on the floor behind my head, he puts his hands under my head with his fingertips just under my occipital bones. I kept saying, 'It hurts! It hurts! It hurts!' and I'm crying and crying and crying."

Karen heard Wayne say, " 'We're going to take these out now. They're going to go off to heaven, off the planet. We are all protected. We are all safe. Michael is here. Raphael is here.' He did protection for all that were present, 'Everyone call in your own angels.' He had his hands on my head and he said, 'Jesus is here. Take them out Michael.' "

"Wayne is the equivalent of when you're in labor and you have horrible labor pains and someone comes and gives you the epidural, and you go, 'Okay, now I'll just sit back and watch the baby come out.' When he arrived, I stopped experiencing the pain and I let it happen; watched it happen."

"When he put his hands on me but before he took the first entity out, my limbs started trembling. My legs were going, and my arms were going as he was holding my head. Then he said, 'Take it out' and it came out and my limbs stopped. That was the fight. My legs shook, my body shook. I calmed down quite a bit. I continued to weep and to cry and he saw that it wasn't all gone. Then my body shook a little bit more and Wayne said, 'Take them all Michael,' and it came out."

Once the entities were out of Karen's body, the voids left where they once resided were cleansed, purified and filled with Love and Light. Wayne felt it was important that her home also be cleansed and asked for Karen's permission to do the work right then; right there.

"Wayne said, 'Let's go into your house. I want to cleanse your house before I send you home. Tell me what your house looks like.' So he goes into my house and he goes into every room and he blessed the house; then he blessed and cleansed everyone in the house and the area where I sleep."

"Throughout the entire time that I was lying on the floor—struggling in the battlefield—I kept saying to people, 'I'm so sorry! I'm so sorry that I'm here doing this to you and that you all have to be here with me. I'm so sorry.' "

"At the end... I said, 'I'm not gonna say I'm sorry, but I want to say thank you and I'm appreciative.' There was this whole '*I got it!*' I got it that I didn't have to be sorry and that all I had to do was be grateful and not sorry. For me that was such a huge difference! When I heard that come out of my mouth I thought, '*Wow! Something really did happen because I'm not even thinking the same way. I've been rewired.*' "

"Someone helped me stand up and I went to the bathroom and I looked in the mirror, and I smiled! And I didn't even feel ironic or stupid or silly for doing it. The person looking back at me—there was no illusion—that was really profound. It was really, really pure and really clear and I just remember sitting there and for the first time in my life feeling absolute peace."

Karen received the usual aftercare guidance to drink a much greater amount of water than usual and be gentle with herself, as though she had just undergone a surgical procedure, because she did. Wayne advised Karen that over the next forty days she would continue to cleanse and heal: and this would raise some difficult emotions for her but that this was all part of the process.

After Karen went home the night of her healing, she woke up her partner to tell him what had happened,

"He sits up, looks at me and he's like, 'You look really different.' We read *Psalms*. I wanted to pray. I was very charged-up spiritually."

"I woke up the next morning and told my mom, and she's going, 'You don't look the same.' People since then have just looked at me and said, 'You look really clear. You don't look the same.' I see it in my own eyes and my family sees it. There's a look of newness, where before you could see in my face there were influences, like a begrudging or a hurt... where emotions have been written. Now there's a blankness, almost. Betsy said it well when she said, 'It's Light. It's formless. It hasn't been formed yet.' Everything's just sort of new. It's not defined."

During this extended forty-day healing process, Karen's whole inner world began to change and she had many discoveries and healing experiences: including a new-found ability to look at, deal with and heal old traumas from childhood.

"I couldn't eat for about a week. I went on a three-day juice diet/fast which was helpful. Then I started eating again. It was cleansing. Within seven days I was eating normal food again but since then I have to pray over my food or it hurts to digest it. If I don't bless it and raise it in vibration I can't digest it; it doesn't feel good. Certain foods I've become even more sensitive to: glutens will bring me down. It's almost as if I've come into an acknowledgement of my true frequency and I'm in harmony with myself without these interfering energies, and so now I have to eat things that are in agreement with that energy too, and I'm learning what those are."

"If I wear something heavy, I feel tired and I feel dragged down. And when I put on the light clothes my frequency goes up and I feel really bright and I have more mental clarity. It's just like the foods: I've always been subtly sensitive to food, clothing and people, but since that healing it's intensified a hundred times. It's become really pronounced and I'm seeing it. I've really become very, very aware of my own energy in a way that I never have before. I know that I was sensitive before, but now there's no distraction and I'm able to see it. I'm able to see how I'm affected by what I wear, and what I eat, and who I talk to. I'm able to see where my energy is going, when I'm reaching a dip; and why. I know what I need to do to get back up."

"I'm able to see certain learned behavioral patterns like intolerance or lack of patience for others, and when it starts to come up I'm able to catch it and see that I have a choice and I'm able to make the choice without the battle, which is awesome! I'm not perfect at it yet—I've had my moments—but it's like the volume was turned way down. I'm still capable of anger, intolerance and frustration, but I'm at a 2 and not a 12, and I can choose to turn it all the way off if I want to. It takes work. You gotta sit and pray and cleanse and make the choice to not be that person, but I feel like I have the power to do it, and that's the big, big difference. Whereas before, I would just grunt, '*I can't stop it!*' The entities really—they control you—they control your feelings. I have a history of violence and I don't feel like I'm that way anymore. I feel really blessed."

"I haven't had sleep paralysis since the healing. A lot of needing to sleep—I had to sleep a lot at first so my subconscious could process what happened, and it did. I had really intense dreams."

"Here's one of the most beautiful things that came out of it: my father isn't active in my life and hasn't been since I was a child. He's a heroin addict and a brilliant musician with a tortured soul, and he lives in another state. My whole life I've had reoccurring dreams of him where I can't get to him. We'll be in a house and he's in one room and I go into the room and he walks away from me. I chase him, and he goes into another room, and I just can't ever get him—or I go to see him and he turns his back on me."

"Four days after Wayne worked on me I had this really healing dream where I was *invited* to his house, and he's lying in bed and he goes, 'Karen! Come here! I love you!' and I get into bed with him—I'm like a little girl—I used to sleep with my parents. I loved cuddling when I was a kid. He said, 'You're such a beautiful child,' and I interpret that as being symbolic of innocence—being born new again. He held me and he said, 'I love you,' and he was so happy to be with me. I woke up and I felt such love and I thought, *'Wow. That's different!'* For me to have a subconscious association of feeling loved from my father—that's a 180."

"My deepest empathy was always for my father. I suffered with him. It just broke my heart to see him hurt and I always took on his pain, and then blamed my mother for it, and never held my dad accountable for anything. I saw him as a saint, even when he hurt me. So there were a lot of unhealthy associations there... I think that that was one of the things that went out... maybe something happened. There may have been an event—and I really wouldn't be surprised if something jumped out of him and went into me—or I offered it, saying, 'Let me take your pain.' I always wanted to save him and suffer for him so he wouldn't suffer. I've been told that I've died to save him in past lives. I'm real convinced that one of those entities came from him and that I offered to take it on."

The miraculous turn-around in Karen's life is something she continues to be grateful for and explore even deeper with the knowledge and joy of being blessed beyond measure by the Light.

SARAH

Sarah found herself born into a family that had an abusive member and beginning at the incomprehensible age of three, was subjected to numerous sexual assaults while growing up. A heavy burden was transferred to her during these attacks and she has been living with the emotional and spiritual consequences of her victimization for her entire life.

Sarah has struggled with eating disorders since childhood and as a result, has been hospitalized four times during her lifetime. She went through lengthy periods of time where she was unable to consume solid foods and subsisted on a liquid diet.

She married a man who was also haunted by forces that he was probably not aware of and he brought greater shadow into Sarah's life until his suicide in 1992. Sarah believes that his death was the result of trying to free himself from his despair and feelings of hopelessness. This was a catalyst for many challenges and difficulties for the loving wife and three children he left behind.

After the death of her beloved husband, Sarah began having thoughts that terrified her, "I could be driving down the road and suddenly I'd get this horrid picture of my son or my grandchild or someone with their head open and bleeding... really extreme things like that...." She called these episodes "catastrophic thinking" and was haunted by them daily.

Desperately seeking relief, Sarah found a loving group of people who were employing methods to help students integrate their many levels of consciousness into a more cohesive, meaningful and harmonious experience. This was a different group than the one she was religiously affiliated with but it brought her great comfort and benefit that her religion couldn't provide.

The newfound group practiced what Sarah describes as, "A deep healing at a level I have never seen before with anything; permanent, vast, takes you to another level in life."

Regular attendance of these conferences over the course of several years was Sarah's mental lifeline. If she missed one, she would lose her grip on keeping her catastrophic thoughts and other negative thinking at bay: they *always* seemed to be amplified under stress and fatigue.

She noticed that other members who had practiced deep healing for shorter periods of time were having results that seemed to far surpass her own but she couldn't figure out what was holding her back, blocking her from taking off like the rocket of Light that she wanted to become.

She expressed her concern this way, "I saw people who got into these conferences long after I did and who excelled a lot faster than me. Sometimes that's frustrating."

Sarah had a seizure while attending one of these conferences that was specifically focused on healing. During her seizure, a facilitator approached Sarah and explained that she had an entity attached to her. The woman asked if Sarah would like it removed and she emphatically replied that she would. Sarah feels that this removal was a success and put an end to the seizure she was having at that moment.

Sarah's seizures originally began at the age of twenty-two, immediately following the birth of her second child. She has had a total of three Cesarean-section births and has had increasing difficulty since the second, relatively routine surgical procedure.

During the Cesarean surgery with her third child, the surgeon left a piece of gauze in her abdomen! This disgusting mistake created chronic illness, pain and auto-immune difficulties that dramatically damaged her cornea and induced a myriad of other symptoms: all of these were likely triggered by the imbalance of her body trying to correct the problem. Sarah also suffered frequent headaches, extreme fatigue, ovarian cysts and hair-loss and as a result, she missed months of work.

In addition to all of these unfortunate circumstances, Sarah found herself continuously harassed by what she perceived as her own mind. The thoughts impressed upon her were continuously self-degrading, which added to her eating disorder and to the depressing sense that she might never find anyone who could love her.

"It affected every relationship I had because my thinking was so different. I lived in a world of guilt and fear: and it just kind of kept reciprocating. I could do things to clear it temporarily but it came back. I felt constantly exhausted from trying—from being on that treadmill of 'I've got to fix this. I've got to keep this up. I've got to do something everyday. I've got to find another conference. I've got to...' the pressure of trying to keep it away was exhausting."

"I got into a very abusive, controlling, manipulative, miserable relationship... because the abusive self-derogatory thoughts were so deep. It had been seven years after my husband died when I got in that relationship. I was involved for way-too-long just because the head talk was so bad and I thought no one was ever going to want me again."

Romantic relationships weren't the only challenges Sarah faced in her life. After the death of her husband, all of her children seemed to experience dramatic shifts in their thought processes and perceptions, "The youngest one still deals with a lot of depression and he has a lot of things holding him back: a lot of self-denigration. He lives in guilt and fear."

"The middle one... she did better after my husband's death in some ways. A couple of years after he committed suicide, she tried to commit suicide using the exact same scenario—she did exactly what he did—except she didn't have access to a car, and he did. She was only fourteen when she tried to kill herself."

"She was hospitalized for a year and got 24-7 care for months, where her thought process was repeatedly and almost immediately altered, so she does better at this point than my boys do, and I think that's why. For months and months and months, twenty-four hours a day—if she woke up for one second, the care worker would immediately get the thoughts transferred and changed. It was definitely a process of clearing that out."

Sarah's oldest son stopped talking to her several years before she saw Wayne for a healing.

Sarah believed that she was led to Wayne through a particularly gifted psychic in Albuquerque named Catherine. This new adviser told her that she had "something attached" and also a form of cancer across her stomach region that would end her life within six months if she did not get help.

"Catherine said I was full of cancer across my abdomen and I do believe that that's true because as a kinesiologist and a naturopath I know that there is a malignancy point, and I could never get it to clear. I would take twenty to thirty supplement capsules with each meal every day just to manage, just to survive to come into work. The malignancy point would get less... but it would go right back... other practitioners were baffled too. I've been to a lot of other practitioners trying to get healing...."

Being a member of a particularly oppressive religious organization made it even harder for Sarah to find help. Spiritually-based counseling or alternative healing methods that had any link with the Divine were discouraged or openly condemned. Any and all connection with God had to be approved by the organization. Any member who went against the rules had to pay a terrible price and seeing someone like Wayne would be cause for great consequence within the group.

"I was terrified when I went to see Wayne because I was so programmed to feel that I was doing something wrong if I thought about any kind of spirit energy or anything. I was terrified and yet at the same time I thought, Catherine was right about everything—she told me I had six months to live—and I knew in my heart, in my soul... she was right."

"I've never been to anybody like Wayne, ever... I would never have done that had I not had that reading with Catherine. It was God-sent."

Sarah had two sessions with Wayne and one of his mentored apprentice associates, Valentina, assisted with the first session. As is standard procedure in sessions with Wayne, Jesus worked from within and Archangels' Michael and Raphael worked from the outside. *In the first session, five entities were removed!*

While Wayne generally feels the presence of entities and negativity, Valentina is able to see them and noticed a swelling in Sarah's head that she described as a gray, shadow figure. This entity was the cause of her confusion, immune system disturbances and seizures. She also saw entity presences on Sarah's shoulder and abdominal area. Sarah reflects upon her experience in the following paragraphs.

"The first one, I knew was coming from the head. It was the one connected to the headaches because I suddenly felt the pain of the headache as Wayne was removing it. It occurred to me that that was the headache one, and it was causing problems with my eyes. I know it was connected with my seizures as well. That's when Valentina said, 'You've been having seizures since you were twenty-two.' There was no way for her to know that."

"Each time Wayne was doing the releases, I new exactly where it was being released from on my body... I knew a lot was connected with my husband. Wayne described what caused my husband to commit suicide: those same entities, which then transferred to me and the children, and I believe that."

During her first session with Wayne, Sarah's husband was present and apologizing profusely for what he had done. He said that he had no idea of the havoc that would ensue after his suicide for himself and his family. If he'd known then, he said, what he knows now, things would have been different. He came to the session to assist in the release of something Sarah was carrying from the relationship. It was deep-rooted and caused her great suffering. He didn't want her to suffer; she was not at fault.

"That's the other thing that I noticed from Wayne's treatment—the last treatment that he did—this last treatment let go of a sexual abuse connected entity and that had been with me since before age three... I felt it go when Wayne did what he did. I pictured the abuser, and the picture that I got was it came out of the abuser into me during a sexual abuse episode. I feel differently about it, I just know something shifted, something changed. There's a sense of my body back."

Sarah had absolutely no knowledge that she had been the host of entities since she was three-years-old. When a person is joined by an entity at a young age, there is little or no way to distinguish the true or original self from the invading presence. One grows up believing that the thoughts and impressions being made by these beings are indeed of their own invention; they believe it is who they truly are.

The results of Sarah's two sessions with Wayne, Jesus, Raphael and Michael proved to be the best thing she could have done for herself. After a total of seven entities were removed, nearly all of Sarah's physical, mental and emotional symptoms have disappeared or have been dramatically reduced.

"Right after I saw Wayne, I was extremely hungry... I felt like I was starving, I had been starving for months but everything had moved down from the upper GI tract—whatever it was opened up and I could eat—and I'm still eating well."

"My hair used to fall out. It's not falling out anymore... I'm a healthcare practitioner, I'm supposed to eat really healthy food and I would... for months on end... and then I'd feel so driven by whatever it was—this force that you just can't stop—and I'd have something very unhealthy for myself."

"I've noticed that I haven't had that urge *at all*... no food has that power over me anymore. One of the entities there definitely had that force that once it hit I couldn't control it... since Wayne, the thinking is not there, the force is not there and I don't feel driven. That's a freedom I could never get."

"I have no headaches, no seizures. The fatigue is nothing like it was. I sleep better. I can eat. Just to be able to eat is such a blessing. The female problems don't feel as bad."

And Sarah's thoughts have become very positive in her once haunted, chattering mind, "It feels different—really different—quiet."

Just weeks before her first visit with Wayne, Sarah explains, "I couldn't read anymore. I suddenly could not read. I couldn't see the words anymore. They were all shaded and the doctor said the cornea was wearing away. They were no longer smooth, they were torn up... my eyes are now recovered too: they're seventy percent better... the eye doctor just confirmed seventy percent better eyes, and that was in just a couple of weeks!"

Sarah also feels that her slower progress in her own avenues of healing and self-improvement have been unblocked, "I feel like what Wayne did was the other key—the piece that was missing for me—I feel that I'm creating a whole new life now."

AARON

As far as Aaron knew, he was living a pretty normal life; busy doing all of the standard, normal things all of us do, and more. Growing up in a European country where personal reflections of spirit were more widely accepted, he had a vague awareness that there were two sides to the spiritual coin from his father. The patriarch of the family always seemed to know when spiritual danger or darkness was lurking and he had a unique ability to identify the source. Aaron's dad had issued a family-wide warning that they were to exercise extra caution around a particular woman with a local reputation for aligning with dark power and he identified her clearly for his wife and children; so Aaron, "...was careful about her... usually."

When he was twenty-six, Aaron's niece walked down the aisle to recite the traditional vows at her wedding and for most of the guests, the reception was a time of great joy and merriment. Everyone was open, some were drinking, some were singing joyfully and in the moment of excited chaos before a toast to the bride and groom, the woman who Aaron had been forewarned to avoid, passed him a small shot-glass of alcohol through another guest. Although Aaron was not intoxicated, he found himself unconscious within minutes, only to be revived by the blazing pain.

Aaron described the impact of that one drink in the following manner, "I wasn't drunk at all before, and it was a small shot: it shouldn't have affected me that much... but I lost my consciousness. I remembered about five minutes and after that I don't remember anything. I regained my consciousness because I started feeling very sharp pain... in the epigastric area, in the middle of my stomach. The pain was so bad that I couldn't breathe. I was thinking that I was dying—I cannot describe it."

While these types of phenomena are difficult to fully explain, a revelation in the future led Aaron to realize that this is the moment that defined his life for the next *twenty years*. At the time, he thought he had been poisoned and tried to induce vomiting and other forms of detoxification. He did not realize how drastically his life was about to change from this incident.

After the wedding, Aaron's life became a struggle, "I didn't expect that it could affect my actual life."

He found that people were responding to him in negative ways, displaying jealousy and resentment. From his perspective, each important decision was carefully weighed but as he proceeded toward implementation, almost everything, every time, would mysteriously backfire on Aaron. It was as if he'd been sabotaged: most of his sincere efforts to improve his own life or that of others were repeatedly thwarted.

Even for a highly educated man like Aaron, who earned a doctorate degree within the field of surgical medicine, work became unpleasant and a distinct sense of living a life controlled by someone else permeated Aaron's consciousness during the next six years.

"I felt like something was affecting my life in a bad way. Having an entity impacts your decisions; it makes you more uncertain about lots of things. You're still alive and keep doing whatever you're doing normally—you're eating, you're sleeping—but it's different. You're constantly getting in some situations that you have not personally created. So many things were going wrong... that life became a struggle. You're making some decisions that are totally wrong for you and then you're asking yourself, *'Why did I do this?'* It's not your decision. It's very illogical. It's very unpredictable. It's not your decision. Period."

"At the same time, I felt like something was hitting me, something was laughing the moment I screwed up. In the situation, it was like something behind me was just laughing at me: 'Ha ha ha! Got you again!' "

"For at least five, maybe six years, I didn't even realize that I was influenced by this; what I came to know later was an entity but I got more and more feelings that something happened—that it was completely not my life, then I became so sad. I was so upset and so disappointed that sometimes I didn't care about life anymore because it was not my life. It was so destructive and I didn't know how to deal with that."

After years of fighting against imbalanced odds, Aaron became convinced that something was wrong and needed to be fixed but what exactly, was wrong? What was at the root of the problem? And who fixes these things? Aaron constantly sought solutions for what plagued him but did not know who to see or where to go. There are specialists for everything from foot fungus to brain tumors but where were the radio ads for healers who help with a sudden loss of control over one's life, and the source of such things?

For many years Aaron searched, "I was looking constantly for some opportunity to find a solution. There were some people who were natural healers but there was no one who would say, 'You have this and this and I will help you to remove it.' "

In his process of searching for ways to grow spiritually and improve the quality of his life, Aaron took some channeling classes with Betsy. He felt a growing discomfort coming from *somewhere* within him as he completed Level-One and then Level-Two of his channeling courses. However, through this course of study, he met Wayne, Valentina and other wonderful people who were also working to connect with the Love of the Divine.

It was clear to Wayne that Aaron was being plagued by an entity; upon closer inspection during the healing session he found that Aaron had been completely roped and bound energetically with hundreds of cords! Wayne described them as one-inch thick, manila-colored ropes that bound Aaron like a mummy. It was no wonder that Aaron was stuck and unable to change his reality into something better! In fact, it was amazing that he could function at all!

With the help of Jesus, Archangel Raphael and Archangel Michael, the entity was removed via Aaron's crown. It had been anchored in his head, neck and upper spine. Valentina was able to psychically see that this entity was witch-like in nature and it attempted to escape the Light by leaping from Aaron into the nearest available host. The protective shields around all of the participants during the healing session with Wayne and his guides quickly thwarted this plan and the entity was permanently removed from the planet.

The entity—while appearing to resemble the "dark woman" who sent it to Aaron via the shot-glass and black magic—was actually a separate, conscious being with its own agenda. It was clear that the entity had entered Aaron's body during his blacked-out, unconscious state and had gained entry with assistance from this woman. However, her motivations for the attack are unknown.

Jesus remained in Aaron's body for the next forty-eight hours, as is often the case after a major healing session that involves the removal of an entity that is demonic in nature. These dark beings take up space within the people that they reside and Jesus often stays for a period of time to fill up that void with Love and Light of a highly Divine frequency and nature.

"I definitely felt something releasing from my body," Aaron recalls.

He also had a sense of the presence, the struggle *between* Light and Darkness during the healing.

Immediately following this major healing, Aaron's body needed to rest; he felt very weak. A day in the mountains proved fruitful for Aaron, allowing him to notice how much better he felt emotionally but the cleansing and healing continued unabated for several weeks and during this period, a number of temporary physical symptoms arose.

The entity within Aaron had been impacting everything. It controlled his spiritual, mental, emotional and physical health: and when the entity was released, it relinquished control of all of those. Aaron began to have a new awareness of what his own body was truly experiencing. What had previously been masked was exposed and Aaron was led to various informative materials to help with his physical ailments: back pains and a temporarily increased susceptibility to minor illnesses such as the common cold.

After the healing, Aaron expressed that he, "Felt like a different me... lots of things started opening for me... I would discover a book, open it and would see something directly related to what I needed."

Aaron found similar experiences in opening his email; he discovered that help for his post-healing physical discomfort was almost literally, being dropped into his lap!

As promised by Wayne, Aaron's physical symptoms were short-lived and his overall health has improved. He describes day-and-night changes in his self-esteem and emotional health. While Aaron still has to face the challenges of everyday living like the rest of us, he has been released from chronic worry. He is much happier and reports that most areas of his life have improved.

Aaron's spiritual progress has gained great momentum. He used to feel interference in his ability to nurture his gifts into wholeness, but Aaron now finds that meditation, prayer and his ability to channel messages of Love and Light have "increased tremendously." As a result, he is able to focus and prioritize without the constant, fearful thoughts fed to him by the entity, thus enabling him to make better, appropriate decisions. He can trust his intuition which has also dramatically increased in its reliability now that he has been permanently freed from the spiritual prison that the entity had built around him.

All that remains for Aaron to conquer during this chapter of his life are a few disconnected cords left behind by the angels as a gift for him. Aaron is learning some valuable lessons and thus benefiting by his work to shrink and ultimately dissolve those cords simply by staying positive and focusing on the Light. A report from Archangel Raphael through Wayne indicates that he is succeeding because they are thinner and weaker than they were when the sword of Archangel Michael cut them.

Aaron sums up his journey beautifully, "To be under control of someone blocking you completely, manipulating your mind... that was a meaningless life. After that, I'm ready for anything."

He happily states, "I feel like I am myself now."

This is the *one* from which we can never run away, but we certainly deserve the chance and the right to know who we truly are and improve ourselves. Thanks to Wayne and his beloved guides, Aaron now has that opportunity.

SPIRIT RELEASEMENT PRACTITIONERS

It was truly an honor to be invited to study Wayne's work and to have the privilege of meeting with and interviewing some of his wonderful clients. It was exhilarating and liberating to listen and watch as they shared their stories: the way their eyes sparkled with excitement when they spoke of their release from the bondage of their possessions. It was a gift to me; a reminder that we are never alone and there is nothing that cannot be overcome by the Love and Light of God.

Within the pages of this book, we have explored some of the ways we attract or invite entities into our lives: using oracular tools such as the Ouija Board ignorantly as was the case with Renee, or blatantly inviting them *in* out of anger and fear like Maria. We've learned that they can be with us from past life experiences or attach to us in times of grief, fear or pain. We can acquire them during surgical procedures or with the use of alcohol or other mood altering substances that damage our auric fields—shields which protect us from outside energies.

We have even seen that these entities can be sent by others utilizing black magic as a catalyst. These intruders can destroy our relationships, mess with our heads and hinder our spiritual evolution. Most importantly, we've learned that there is *never* a benevolent outcome from their presence: once they're *in* we need assistance to remove them and they can destroy the quality of our lives and inner worlds when they're allowed to linger.

It is frequently expressed that if a more holistic approach to healing was taken; if all traditions of medicine and healing would be open to working with other traditions; there would be a significantly better outcome in substantially more cases. If segments of society could admit that they hold just one piece of the puzzle, there would be far less tragedy and a lot more healing that would occur for the myriads of people suffering all over the world.

In the cases where health problems are being caused by the long-term residence of an entity, it may be true that the host requires traditional care or surgery but this is just a treating of symptoms rather than a cure for the source of the problem. This is comparable to having a cancerous tumor removed from a lung but continuing to smoke... it probably will not end well.

A person with a long-standing mental or emotional imbalance may benefit to some degree by the use of medications that are manufactured to correct the chemical imbalances of the brain but if there is an entity constantly feeding negativity or grotesque images into that person's mind and it is allowed to continue, there will be nothing but a partial reduction of the symptoms while the body of that person continues to carry a generator of pain and sorrow.

It is exciting to learn that there are alternative options for those of us that have exhausted traditional Western methods of treatment to cure what ails us! It may simply be that we have been under the sinister influence of entities and attachments that have played a major role in robbing us of our self-love, inner peace and even our physical health.

Now that you have read several detailed accounts of those who were under the control of a variety of dark forces and the benefits they received from Divine Healings, it is time to describe and divulge who can perform these healings safely and how you may discern the right healer for you.

First, we urge that you *do not try this at home*! If not implemented or administered correctly, healings can go horribly wrong for every-body. It is absolutely necessary to find an experienced spirit releasement practitioner to perform these removals safely and effectively.

There are many healers who are presently performing these removals but do not discuss it publicly because it's not their intention to release entities, and they have not been taught that this could be a natural result of a session involving energy work of any kind. When these unexpected releases occur, these practitioners may not know how to send these beings into the Light for healing or how to protect themselves or their clients against possession.

Even worse, some well intentioned but inexperienced healers do this work from their own homes; with others living in the house. They may inadvertently free these entities within their living space and everyone in the house becomes jeopardized, especially little ones—children—who are so open, so vulnerable to receiving and not taught how to protect themselves.

It is important for practitioners to be involved in some form of community or relationship with others in their field. It is crucial that they begin to share their experiences of entity removals regardless of the type of healing work they perform. If they spoke of this openly, they would discover that a large percentage of their fellow practitioners have encountered these forces during a session. Many of them do not know how to handle this phenomenon safely. A network of learning needs to be established, all healers should know what to do when this issue arises, because it will!

There are surprisingly few practitioners with the qualifications and education to do this work safely, properly and completely. And those who are unqualified may suffer greatly for their attempts to assist. Entity removal is a specialty. If you have a potentially fatal disease such as cancer, do you see your child's pediatrician? Of course not! You go to an oncologist because this kind of healer *specializes* in your infirmity. This is only logical.

The entities that are released must be sent to the Light to be healed. If they are not, they will immediately seek to return to their host or find a new host. This could be the practitioner, or anyone else nearby. It is dangerously counterproductive.

When entities are removed, there is a void in the space they once occupied and this must be filled with Love and Light. Some practitioners are removing entities and are not aware that their client is left with an empty space that housed all of the negativity; it needs to be cleansed and filled for the healing to be complete.

There is a tremendous amount of knowledge involved in the sacred art form of spirit releasement. The practitioner must take the time to cleanse and protect themselves and their space, as well as anyone nearby. While there are many methods for accomplishing this, some are more powerful than others and summoning all of the appropriate spiritual parties is vital to the safety and well-being of everyone involved.

Some practitioners also protect their clients by sending Spirit Guides or Angels directly to them so that any attempted interference by entities is thwarted and the host arrives safely for their appointment at the scheduled time. Once the healing is successfully completed, the practitioner again must cleanse and protect their clients and themselves.

Entity releasement can be done long-distance. Much of this work can be accomplished without regard for time and space because it takes place on a spiritual plane of existence. If you do not have a qualified healer in your area, one in another state—or even in another country—is capable of assisting you in most cases. Do not go to someone inexperienced in spirit releasement just because they live nearby!

If you believe you may have an entity possession, there is no cause for alarm but there is a call to action! A great place to begin is on Wayne Brewer's Web site: www.AreYouPossessed.net Here you will find answers to frequently asked questions, resources and contact information to schedule a Divine Healing!

TRUE FREEDOM

Entities are like shadows that block the Sun, that hover between you and the sky. It is time for you to soar! So much joy, peace, love and beauty await each and every one of you, and it is time that you claim it for yourself!

There should be no shame now; only joy—joy—because you have finally found your answers! You finally discovered the word tools to allow you to speak definitively of this phenomenon, that you may find the healers who can facilitate the removal of these inconvenient flu bugs, these entities.

It is time to bring this epidemic into the open. It is time to talk about it, time to notice: That is not my thought. I feel stagnant; I try to expand my consciousness but can't move forward. Why? Where did that gruesome image come from? That is not who I am! If it is not from love, it is not who you are! It is time to start asking questions and comparing notes because these beings take refuge, they find shelter amidst the secrecy and fear. If there were no place to hide, no silence, no shame, then there would be a massive healing transforming this planet in a very short period of time.

You now realize that there is nothing to be frightened of; after all, if you have entity possessions they have come to you for your strength, energy and power. What does that tell you about yourself? It should tell you that you are a powerful, creative being of Light whose natural state is one of love, not fear.

Fear can be a powerful obstacle but it doesn't have to be. In every single moment you get to choose: Love or Fear. Each time you choose Love, you begin to starve the entity and begin to raise your frequency, which in turn makes it highly uncomfortable for the dark beings relying on your fear. They feed on negativity; you can choose not to feed them!

Please remember that the entities you may carry are conscious and intelligent. They do not want you to receive the Divine grace of God and be healed—they would lose their host and be sent into the Light... and they fear this tremendously. Not until they get to the other side do they realize what they had become and begin to evolve into their next phase of evolution. They too receive Divine grace! Be aware that they may place blocks in your path, like empty gas tanks that were full the prior evening or intense traffic congestion and construction when you decide you wish to be healed. Do not let this frighten you, for it is but a game, a last resort, a fear tactic to prevent their removal.

It is time for you to recognize yourself. You are powerful, and do not even know it! If you could only see the truth of who you are, you would have no fear, no shame and no challenges from entities, for you would see the grand nature of your infinite being—

your soul—and you would rejoice! Rejoice in knowing that there are no low frequency beings that can harm you. Until that day comes, and it will, go see someone for a Divine Healing, then learn to channel and bring forth higher energies of Love and Light, and you will know the grace of God firsthand in a very tangible way.

A unique time is approaching when humanity will not rely on pain to grow. You can choose to begin making this reality yours now by gifting yourself with the freedom that is your birthright: freedom from possession and interference, freedom from the cords and ropes that bind your spirit to the past. It is yours. It is yours for the asking. Yours for the taking! Are you ready to receive? God is ready to give, so open your eyes and your heart and prepare for your world to expand in new, benevolent and profound ways!

Resources

www.AreYouPossessed.net
Wayne Brewer

www.PsychicCelebrations.com
Arianna Nappi

www.AskBetsyMorgan.com
Betsy-Morgan Coffman

www.ValentinaAragon.com
Valentina Aragon

www.Abraham-Hicks.com
The Law of Attraction

Author Information

Wayne Brewer is a prominent Private Investigator with over 34 years of experience uncovering hidden truths. Putting his P.I skills to use in the spiritual arena, he has discovered an ability and technique for effective removal of dark, demonic and/or disincarnate spirits that are displaced. He currently utilizes these gifts and techniques in his Albuquerque-based spirit releasement practice. His experience performing both in-person and long-distance sessions has provided an abundance of inspiration and information to assist anyone on the journey to spiritual wellness.

Arianna Nappi is a professional writer, psychic, channel, and energy healer in Albuquerque, NM. Certified in the Orion Technologies, she teaches nationally available channeling classes and local channeled workshops on a variety of spiritual topics. She is available for private sessions locally and long-distance.

CPSIA information can be obtained
at www.ICGtesting.com
Printed in the USA
FFOW02n1705230817